The Day of Worship

The Day of Worship

Reassessing the Christian Life in Light of the Sabbath

Ryan M. McGraw

Reformation Heritage Books
Grand Rapids, Michigan

The Day of Worship
© 2011 by Ryan M. McGraw

Reformation Heritage Books
2965 Leonard St. NE
Grand Rapids, MI 49525
616-977-0889 / Fax 616-285-3246
orders@heritagebooks.org
www.heritagebooks.org

Printed in the United States of America
11 12 13 14 15 16/10 9 8 7 6 5 4 3 2 1

Library of Congress Cataloging-in-Publication Data

McGraw, Ryan M.
The day of worship : reassessing the Christian life in light of the Sabbath / Ryan M. McGraw.
    p. cm.
Includes bibliographical references and index.
ISBN 978-1-60178-155-0 (pbk. : alk. paper)
1. Sunday. 2. Sabbath. 3. Worship. 4. God (Christianity)—Worship and love. 5. Reformed Church—Doctrines. I. Title.
BV111.3.M36 2011
263'.3—dc23
                                    2011041891

For additional Reformed literature, both new and used, request a free book list from Reformation Heritage Books at the above regular or e-mail address.

This book is
dedicated to my wife,
Krista,

and to
"the boys."

CONTENTS

ACKNOWLEDGMENTS

Particular thanks are due to Pastor Wade Whitcomb for gently rebuking my Sabbath-breaking when I was a young believer many years ago and for directing me to Dr. Pipa's book on the Lord's Day. I am grateful to Dr. Joseph Pipa for being a father and mentor in the faith, one whose family exemplifies joyful Sabbath-keeping. Your ministry to my soul has meant more to me than I can express. The editorial team at Reformation Heritage Books improved the work greatly through many very useful stylistic suggestions. My heartfelt appreciation goes to Jay Collier, director of publications for RHB, for taking interest in my work and for his continual encouragement. Dr. Joel Beeke has helped me greatly as a writer, a minister, and a Christian by his winsome presentation of the truth, his love for experimental piety, his humility, and his kindness. Dr. Beeke has given great assistance and encouragement, not only on this project but also in connection to numerous other articles and endeavors. My mother-in-law, Sylvia Stevens, has generously devoted her time and care in giving me excellent editorial suggestions. If I have achieved some measure of clarity in my writing, then it is largely due to what I have learned from her. Thanks to Grace Presbyterian Church, in Conway, South Carolina, for sitting under a large part of the teaching presented in this book. My prayer is that this material would profit the souls of each member of this beloved congregation. Lastly, my wife, Krista, is my greatest earthly encouragement and blessing in all of my labors. She is my best companion and my greatest joy apart from the triune God. Thank you for reading through this book with me and for strengthening my hands for ministry through your prayers and your fellowship.

Ultimately, if there is anything profitable in this work, then may all honor go to the Father, the Son, and the Holy Spirit. Lord, bless the writing of this book and be glorified by blessing the church in reading it with great benefit.

INTRODUCTION

As a new believer, I had not given particular attention to the fourth commandment, or Sabbath day. I was shocked when a minister told me that not only should I refrain from my worldly employments on the Sabbath day, but that I should abstain from recreations and conversation that would be lawful on other days. He also taught me that the Sabbath was designed by God to be a day in which the entire time was to be spent in the joyful duties of public and private worship, which is meant to be a foretaste of heaven itself. Since then, after I weighed the biblical evidence as to how the Christian Sabbath or Lord's Day should be kept, it has proved to be the best day of the week and the "market day of the soul," with exceedingly great and precious promises attached to it.

The distinctive feature of this book is that it demonstrates the Sabbath was designed to be sanctified for the purpose of worship, and this is the primary factor that should give shape to its practical observance. There was a time in which Presbyterians, Baptists, Methodists, Congregationalists, and even some Anglicans and Dutch Reformed shared a fundamental unity on how the Lord's Day, or Christian Sabbath, should be kept. All of these denominations held in common what is today referred to as the Puritan view of the Sabbath. The Westminster Shorter Catechism has set forth this view: "The Sabbath is to be sanctified by an holy resting all that day, even from such worldly employments and recreations as are lawful on other days, and by taking up the entire time in the public and private exercises of God's worship, except so much as is to be taken up in the works of necessity and mercy" (Question 61). Today many have dismissed this viewpoint out of hand as unwarranted from Scripture, legalistic, and inconsistent with the gospel of our Lord Jesus Christ. Even in Reformed churches, most people today have never heard a biblical defense for this position in all its parts. My purpose in the pages that follow is to present the biblical foundations for the particulars of Sabbath-keeping as set forth in the Westminster Standards. The style of the work is homiletical and is presented in the familiar style and direct address of a series of sermons.

There are a few recent books on Sabbath-keeping that have done an excellent job defending the basic tenets of this position. However, many have read these works and remained unconvinced. The material in this book has resulted from over ten years of study and interaction with church members. I have sought to approach the issues related to Sabbath-keeping in a manner that has satisfied the consciences of many by addressing the biblical foundations for the Westminster position from an angle different from other authors. For this reason, the material in this work has very little overlap with, for example, the excellent books by Joseph Pipa, Walter Chantry, and Iain Campbell.[1] I have sought to address what I believe to be the primary underlying issues behind the widespread neglect of the Sabbath day.

For this reason, chapters 1 and 2 address the importance of Sabbath-keeping in Scripture. I contend that the importance of the question has largely been underestimated by the modern Reformed community. By beginning with the importance of Sabbath-keeping in Scripture, I intend to set the tone for the rest of the book by awakening the church to the importance of the issue so that she may study it with eagerness and with a listening ear and a ready heart.

Chapters 3 and 4 are an attempt to examine the factors that affect the proper interpretation of Isaiah 58:13–14:

---

1. Joseph A. Pipa, *The Lord's Day* (Fearn, U.K.: Christian Focus, 1996); Walter Chantry, *Call the Sabbath a Delight* (Edinburgh: Banner of Truth, 1991); Iain Campbell, *On the First Day of the Week: God, the Christian, and the Sabbath* (Leominster, U.K.: Day One, 2005).

> If thou turn away thy foot from the sabbath, from doing thy pleasure on my holy day; and call the sabbath a delight, the holy of the LORD, honourable; and shalt honour him, not doing thine own ways, nor finding thine own pleasure, nor speaking thine own words: then shalt thou delight thyself in the LORD; and I will cause thee to ride upon the high places of the earth, and feed thee with the heritage of Jacob thy father: for the mouth of the LORD hath spoken it.

This text is often central to debates over Sabbath-keeping. Too often the entire matter stands or falls with the exposition of this passage. Opponents propose alternative interpretations, but it is rare that either side deals with the underlying theological and contextual issues that have determined their conclusions. I have attempted to provide a more comprehensive treatment of these two factors with respect to this useful and important passage. At the end of this chapter I have included a section on the role of the Sabbath in the revival and reformation of the church.

In chapters 5 and 6, I maintain that our aversion to Sabbath-keeping is not always an exegetical or theological problem, but rather a symptom of the greater problem of worldliness that has entered into the church. The implications and applications of this chapter reach far beyond the Sabbath day and cause us to reflect on the entirety of our Christian lives and how we view the world in which we live.

Chapter 7 then proceeds to establish the practices of Sabbath-keeping from a Reformed view of the law of God. In this chapter, I demonstrate that even if Isaiah 58 had never been written, Sabbath-keeping would touch our thoughts, speech, and recreations, as well as our ordinary labor. I have used Jesus and the apostles as models for how the law of God should be interpreted and applied in the Christian life. Chapter 8 introduces some miscellaneous practical helps.

The next question that ordinarily arises from the Reformed (and biblical) view of the law of God is the charge of legalism. In chapter 9, therefore, I examine the nature of legalism, its causes, and remedies. Readers may perhaps be surprised that I argue (with the help of Thomas Boston) that the *lax* views of Sabbath-keeping, as well as the rest of the commandments of God, are at times symptomatic of legalistic views of the gospel. I maintain that the Reformed view of the relationship between the law and the gospel is largely being lost among Reformed churches presently. Once again, the Sabbath is the symptom of a broader disease.

The last chapter (chapter 10) presents an *a posteriori* argument for Sabbath-keeping by connecting the Sabbath to the biblical picture of heaven. In rounding out the examination of the Christian Sabbath in this manner, I hope to demonstrate that the Westminster, or Puritan, view of the Sabbath is based upon sound exegesis of Scripture, is demanded by a biblical view of the relation to the law and the gospel, and is a consistent expression of how believers ought to view their relation to this world and the world to come.

This work is not designed to be a replacement to the other works mentioned above, but a supplement to them. For this reason and for the sake of brevity I have omitted arguments that the Sabbath is a perpetually binding commandment as well as the change of the day from the seventh to the first day of the week. If any who read this book are not already convinced of the perpetuity of the Sabbath, then I urge them to begin with the excellent article by B. B. Warfield contained in appendix 1. Appendix 2 contains my review of a book that represents a significant attack upon both the principles and practice of Sabbath-keeping: *Keeping the Sabbath Today* by Jay Adams.

This book is about much more than the Sabbath. If after reading it you are not convinced that the Sabbath should be sanctified to the Lord as a sacred day of worship, I will be disappointed. However, if *all* I do is convince you that you must set apart the Sabbath for worship, then I have failed in my purpose entirely. This book addresses much more significant issues, such as the kind of obedience required by the gospel, the relation of the believer to an unbelieving world, the relationship between the law and the gospel, and the focus of our hope of eternal life. It is my prayer that the Lord would use this work to redirect the thoughts of many in these fundamental areas, even if they are not convinced of the Westminster position on the Sabbath.

Whatever you may find in this book that is profitable to your soul, may you give all thanks and glory to God for it. May the great Lord of the Sabbath be pleased to use these pages to restore His day to the blessed purposes for which He designed it.

CHAPTER ONE

The General Importance of the Sabbath

For much of the twentieth century, many people smoked cigarettes on a regular basis. Hardly anyone thought about the harmful effects that might result from the practice. Today, however, things have changed to the degree that society has swung to the opposite extreme. In most places, the use of all tobacco products is virtually forbidden in public, and many scorn even a legitimate and moderate use of them. It is often the case that harmful practices are taken for granted by the masses with no suspicion that these practices are threatening to kill an entire generation. In the nineteenth century, John Brown of Haddington wrote: "Is Sabbath breaking a very horrible crime?—A. Yes; it is a sin against great love, and the source of many other sins; God commanded a man to be stoned to death for gathering sticks on the Sabbath; and hath threatened and destroyed nations for the breach of it."[1]

We live in a time of crisis with respect to Sabbath-keeping. Even considering the barest minimum application of Sabbath-keeping (that we should refrain from our regular employments on the day), most professing Christians will readily agree to work on the Sabbath if requested. Some do so with a sense of uneasiness, but they are nevertheless willing to sacrifice conscience to the pressures of employers. They often receive encouragement from their churches to do so. Many do not self-consciously make Sabbath-keeping a

---

1. John Brown, *Questions & Answers on the Shorter Catechism* (1846; repr., Grand Rapids: Reformation Heritage Books, 2006), 235.

matter of worship and obedience to the Lord, even though they take
it for granted that the fourth commandment is still binding upon
believers. These symptoms reveal that most Christians underestimate the importance Scripture attaches to Sabbath-keeping. They
are also symptoms of more fundamental problems, which will be
addressed later in this book. For this reason, I have not begun this
book with the *profit* of Sabbath-keeping. In Scripture, Sabbath-
breaking is presented as one of the greatest causes of the weakness
of the church and serves as a lightning rod that attracts the judgment of God to churches and nations. When the church has largely
neglected a practice that fosters such devastating consequences, she
incurs the loss of great blessings. The return of these blessings, however, often begins by sounding an alarm.

My purpose in this chapter is earnestly to plead with you to study
the matter of Sabbath-keeping in light of the importance attached to
it in the Scriptures. The Sabbath is not a peripheral issue, but rather
a matter of great importance to the well-being and prosperity of the
church. The importance of the Sabbath is demonstrated by its place
among creation ordinances, because it is a sign of the covenant of
grace, because of its frequent mention in Scripture (particularly the
prophets), because of its relation to Israel's exile, and because of its
purpose as a day of worship.

The Creation Ordinance
Students of geometry ordinarily begin by memorizing certain axioms that are fundamental to working out the equations in their
homework assignments. "Axioms" are fundamental principles that
are meant to guide and govern our thoughts and practices in a given
area. When God placed Adam and Eve in the garden of Eden, He
gave them a few basic principles that would be fundamental to their
lives in this world, and, as a consequence, to all of their posterity
after them. These principles are often referred to as "creation ordinances," and they are woven into the very fabric of this world. They
are a part of God's purposes in creation and will endure as long as

the world as we know it exists. Creation ordinances are independent of any written law of God and even independent of any consideration of the fall of man and of redemption. God's creation ordinances are marriage, labor, and the Sabbath day. I will illustrate the nature and importance of creation ordinances by looking at marriage. God instituted marriage in order to provide Adam with close human companionship in the garden. By appealing to this creation ordinance in particular, Jesus illustrated the importance of creation ordinances in general and what inferences we should draw from them. When the Pharisees questioned Jesus about the lawfulness of divorce and remarriage, He based His positive instruction on marriage on a basic principle with far-reaching consequences. He rooted His teaching on the nature of marriage as a creation ordinance. He said, "Have ye not read, that he which made them at the beginning made them male and female, and said, For this cause shall a man leave father and mother, and shall cleave to his wife: and they twain shall be one flesh? Wherefore they are no more twain, but one flesh. What therefore God hath joined together, let not man put asunder" (Matt. 19:4–6). After the Pharisees objected, Jesus summarized the bottom line of His argument against divorce by saying, "From the beginning it was not so" (v. 8). His argument was essentially this: Every ordinance that God instituted at creation is perpetually binding upon the practices of mankind; marriage was instituted at creation as an indissoluble bond between one man and one woman; therefore, marriage must always be an indissoluble bond between one man and one woman, as long as the creation remains. To violate what God has woven into the very fabric of creation is to strike at the axiomatic principles that God designed perpetually to govern human life in this world. This is why in relation to marriage, God says unequivocally that He "hates divorce," since it violates the "institution which he loves" (Mal. 2:16, 11 [my translation]).

The Sabbath is a creation ordinance as well. In Genesis 2:1–3, it is written: "Thus the heavens and the earth were finished, and all the host of them. And on the seventh day God ended his work which

he had made; and he rested on the seventh day from all his work
which he had made. And God blessed the seventh day, and sanctified it: because that in it he had rested from all his work which God
created and made." That God sanctified the seventh day means He
set it apart as holy. When God gave the Ten Commandments, He
appealed to this sanctification to enforce the reason His people must
keep the Sabbath day. They must sanctify the Sabbath to keep it holy
because God sanctified it to keep it holy when He created the world.
The Sabbath was not instituted when God gave the Ten Commandments; the Ten Commandments enforced the example that God set
at the beginning and that was binding from the inception of life on
earth.[2] This means that violating the Sabbath is on par with violating the institution of marriage or labor. The Sabbath is a part of the
world God has created. To trample it underfoot is to declare that we
would overturn the weekly order that God has woven into the very
fiber of creation. Sabbath-keeping is as integral to man's life as marriage and labor. To violate ordinances that predate and stand apart
from the Fall, and even from redemption in Christ, is to attack the
authority of God as our creator in the most fundamental sense. For
those who treat the Sabbath as though it may be lightly disregarded,
I reply with Jesus, "From the beginning it was not so."

A Sign of the Covenant of Grace

The place of the Sabbath day as a creation ordinance is enough to
highlight the greatness of the sin of Sabbath-breaking. That the Sabbath became a sign of the covenant of grace as well raises the sin of
Sabbath-breaking to horrific proportions.

---

2. See John Murray, *Principles of Conduct: Aspects of Biblical Ethics* (Grand
Rapids: Eerdmans, 1957), 30–35. For the sake of brevity, I am assuming my
reader agrees that the Sabbath is a perpetually binding creation ordinance.
My point is not the perpetuity of the Sabbath, but rather the importance of the
Sabbath. For the fact that the Sabbath is perpetually binding, see Murray and
the article by Warfield appended to this volume.

The exodus brought a significant addition to Sabbath-keeping. Prior to this time, all of creation was expected to keep the Sabbath because God had sanctified the seventh day from the beginning of the world. Israel was therefore expected to remember the Sabbath as a creation ordinance even before the Ten Commandments were pronounced from Mount Sinai (Ex. 16). In Exodus 20:11, God's people were commanded to remember God's work at creation and to follow His example as they continued to keep the Sabbath. In Deuteronomy 5, however, they were instructed to " keep" (v. 12) the Sabbath for a different reason: "And remember that thou wast a servant in the land of Egypt, and that the LORD thy God brought thee out thence through a mighty hand and by a stretched out arm: therefore the LORD thy God commanded thee to keep the sabbath day" (v. 15). Although God through Moses did not claim that the Sabbath had its origins in the exodus, He did attach to it a new significance. All men must keep the Sabbath because God is their creator, but God's people must keep it because He is their redeemer as well.

Although God had promised Abraham that Israel should be His people, there is a sense in which He purchased them to be His people through the exodus (Deut. 32:6). They were delivered from bondage to the Egyptians by passing through the Red Sea. The wrath of God came upon their enemies so Israel might be delivered. Yet there is more to this deliverance than simple freedom from slavery. Israel was delivered from the wrath and curse of God Himself. At the first Passover, the blood of a lamb had to be placed over the doors of each home in Israel if those inside were to be delivered from the destroying angel. In other words, Israel not only had to be delivered from the Egyptians but also from the wrath of their God. Immediately after passing safely through the Red Sea, God reiterated that the greatest danger the people faced was still His own wrath and curse. He said: "If thou wilt diligently hearken to the voice of the LORD thy God, and wilt do that which is right in his sight, and wilt give ear to his commandments, and keep all his statutes, I will put none of these diseases upon thee, which I have brought upon the Egyptians, for I am the LORD that healeth thee" (Ex. 15:26). The people had been redeemed from the land of Egypt and the house of bondage, but their redemption had not ultimately and finally delivered them from the threat of the wrath of God. In this connection, it is significant that the apostle Paul referred to Christ as our Passover, who was sacrificed for us (1 Cor. 5:7). The exodus added redemptive significance to the Sabbath, yet this redemption was incomplete in its effects. The full redemptive significance of both the exodus and the Sabbath day is found in the redemption from sin and from the wrath of God that was purchased by Jesus Christ. He is the Lamb of God who takes away the sin of the world (John 1:29).

When God chose the Sabbath to be a sign of redemption that is ultimately found in Christ, He made it a sign of the covenant of grace, which was ratified in Christ's blood (Heb. 9:15–17). God indicated this clearly in Exodus 31:13–16:

> Verily my sabbaths ye shall keep: for it is a sign between me and you throughout your generations; that ye may know that I am the LORD that doth sanctify you. Ye shall keep the sabbath, therefore, for it is holy unto you: every one that defileth it shall surely be put to death: for whosoever doeth any work therein, that soul shall be cut off from amongst his people.... Wherefore the children of Israel shall keep the sabbath, to observe the sabbath throughout their generations, for a perpetual covenant.

At the creation, the Lord had sanctified *the Sabbath*; now the Sabbath would serve as a sign that the Lord had sanctified *the people*, by virtue of a covenantal relationship. When the church neglects the Sabbath, is it not an implicit declaration that she has not been sanctified by the Lord to be His people? Why do we refuse to treasure the day that is a sign that the Lord has sanctified us to be His people by the covenant of grace?[3] When we remember the Sabbath, it is a

---

3. In 1853, the General Assembly of the Presbyterian Church USA boldly declared, "A church without the Sabbath is apostate; a people who habitually desecrate this divine institution have abandoned one of the grand foundations of social order and political freedom." Cited by Thomas Peck, *The Works of Thomas Peck* (1895; repr., Edinburgh: Banner of Truth, 1999), 1:195. Whatever you think about this statement, part of the reasoning behind it is that the

perpetual reminder to us that the Lord of the Sabbath is the one who has set us apart to be His people through the blood of the everlasting covenant (Heb. 13:20). The Westminster Larger Catechism summarizes the significance of Sabbath-keeping by stating that the Sabbath is designed "to continue a thankful remembrance of the two great benefits of creation and redemption, which contain a short abridgement of religion" (Q&A 121).

Does this not underscore the seriousness of neglecting the Sabbath? If God will punish those who violate His creation ordinances, will He not much more punish those who trample His redemption underfoot? Bruce Ray writes, "As a sign of grace, the Sabbath declares that salvation depends upon the power of God and not human works. Anyone who worked on the Sabbath day effectively denied that God is the Creator and symbolically rejected salvation by grace."[4] Is it a small thing to break a commandment that is designed to put our minds in remembrance of the covenant that God has made with us in Christ? When we see a rainbow in the sky, we should be mindful of the promises of grace that God gave to Noah; when the Sabbath comes every week, we should be mindful of the redemption from Egypt and the manner in which it pointed to the greater redemption in Christ Jesus our Lord. Many struggle with the law that people were to be put to death for Sabbath-breaking in the Old Testament. Yet in light of the connection of the Sabbath to the glorious plan of salvation, do you not see why men were put to death for such a crime? What is at stake presently is not simply a matter of working one Sunday in order to avoid making employers uncomfortable and

---

world is predominantly dependent upon the means of grace that are exercised on the Sabbath for its knowledge of the gospel of Jesus Christ, and a church that denies the Sabbath day is implicitly rejecting the covenant of grace, of which the Sabbath is a sign. Imagine the violent reaction that would arise if a statement such as this one were even mentioned at the General Assembly of one of the major American Presbyterian denominations today! This shows how far the pendulum has swung in the opposite direction with respect to the church's attitude toward Sabbath-keeping.

4. Bruce A. Ray, *Celebrating the Sabbath: Finding Rest in a Restless World* (Philipsburg, N.J.: P&R, 2000), 36.

acting as though God will sweep Sabbath-breaking under the rug. Whether a person breaks the Sabbath knowingly or not, the widespread neglect of the Sabbath today actually demonstrates a form of contempt for the covenant of grace. You may not have thought of Sabbath-breaking in this manner before, but I plead with those who have sinned in ignorance to hear the Word of God and turn from their ways.

The Frequency of the Sabbath in Scripture

As a young believer, I remember being astonished while listening to the late John H. Gerstner give a series of lectures on the Sabbath. What astonished me at the time was that in one particular lecture, Dr. Gerstner proceeded simply to read a list of direct quotations from Scripture relating to Sabbath-keeping. The sheer number of biblical passages dealing with the subject, coupled with the solemnity inherent in the passages, made an impression upon me I will never forget. When anything in the Scriptures is repeated often, it should demand our attention. The Hebrew term for Sabbath is mentioned in at least 159 verses in the Old Testament. There is a higher concentration of occurrences in Exodus (20 verses) and Leviticus (20 verses), as well as in Isaiah (15 verses), Jeremiah (10 verses), and Ezekiel (28 verses). In the Pentateuch, references to the Sabbath appear so frequently that at times it is difficult to discern the connection they bear to the immediate context. I can provide only a few examples here. After the giving of the Ten Commandments in Exodus 20, the Lord repeated the command to keep the Sabbath in chapter 23 as a preface to the instructions regarding the observance of Israel's annual feasts. As we have seen in the preceding section, the Sabbath appears again in chapter 31 as a sign of God's special relation to His people. In Leviticus 19:3, the Sabbath is inserted in a surprising connection: "Ye shall fear every man his mother, and his father, and keep my sabbaths: I am the LORD your God." In Leviticus 26:2, the Sabbath is connected to corporate worship and serves as a preface to the blessings and curses of the covenant: "Ye shall

keep my Sabbaths, and reverence my sanctuary: I am the LORD."
In Numbers 15:32–36, the Sabbath is used as a case study to demonstrate the consequences of presumptuous sins (see vv. 30–31).
When we read the Pentateuch, we must either conclude that Moses
inserted the Sabbath law randomly throughout these books, or that
the Lord intended to place great emphasis upon the fact that His
people must take special care to remember the Sabbath.

The significance of the Sabbath, however, shines forth the most
clearly in the writings of the prophets. When someone breaks the
law in our country and his court date arrives, a prosecuting attorney relentlessly pursues him. The role of a prosecuting attorney is
to hold the actions of the offender against the law of the land, in
order that he may demonstrate the offender's guilt under the law. In
a similar manner, the prophets of the Old Testament did not make
laws, but rather served as the prosecution, representing God and
enforcing His law against His backsliding people. Isaiah highlighted
the great importance of the prophetic role of calling the people to
return to the law of God when he said, "To the law and to the testimony: if they speak not according to this word, it is because there
is no light in them" (Isa. 8:20). The references to the Sabbath among
the prophets are impressive; they lay great stress on the importance
of the question of Sabbath-keeping.

For the sake of brevity, we will restrict our attention at this
time to one passage from Jeremiah and one from Ezekiel.[5] Jeremiah
17:19–27 states:

> Thus said the LORD unto me; Go and stand in the gate of the
> children of the people, whereby the kings of Judah come in,
> and by the which they go out, and in all the gates of Jerusalem;
> and say unto them, Hear ye the word of the LORD, ye kings
> of Judah, and all Judah, and all the inhabitants of Jerusalem,
> that enter in by these gates: Thus saith the LORD; Take heed to

---

5. For a more extensive treatment of the role of the Sabbath in the teaching of the prophets, see Campbell, *On the First Day of the Week*, 74–102. For a
shorter treatment, see O. Palmer Robertson, *The Christ of the Prophets* (Phillipsburg, N.J.: P&R, 2004), 152–54.

yourselves, and bear no burden on the sabbath day, nor bring
it in by the gates of Jerusalem; neither carry forth a burden
out of your houses on the sabbath day, neither do ye any work,
but hallow ye the sabbath day, as I commanded your fathers.
But they obeyed not, neither inclined their ear, but made their
neck stiff, that they might not hear, nor receive instruction.
And it shall come to pass, if ye diligently hearken unto me,
saith the LORD, to bring in no burden through the gates of
this city on the sabbath day, but hallow the sabbath day, to do
no work therein; then shall there enter into the gates of this
city kings and princes sitting upon the throne of David, rid-
ing in chariots and on horses, they, and their princes, the men
of Judah, and the inhabitants of Jerusalem: and this city shall
remain for ever. And they shall come from the cities of Judah,
and from the places about Jerusalem, and from the land of
Benjamin, and from the plain, and from the mountains, and
from the south, bringing burnt offerings, and sacrifices, and
meat offerings, and incense, and bringing sacrifices of praise,
unto the house of the LORD. But if ye will not hearken unto
me to hallow the sabbath day, and not to bear a burden, even
entering in at the gates of Jerusalem on the sabbath day; then
will I kindle a fire in the gates thereof, and it shall devour the
palaces of Jerusalem, and it shall not be quenched.

For the details of what was probably in view with respect to not
bringing burdens through the gates, see the discussion of Nehemiah
13 that follows. In a day in which Sabbath-breaking is considered a
light or excusable sin with few consequences, we must take special
note of the heights of blessings this passage attaches to Sabbath-
keeping, and the depths of the dreadful curse attached to breaking
God's holy day. Sabbath-breaking is depicted as kindling a fire that
devours everything in its path. It is tempting for many to try to
escape this passage by stating that its regulations were a part of the
Old Testament economy that are no longer relevant for New Testament believers. However, how can we prove legitimately that these
injunctions are types and shadows that represented and pointed to
the Christ who was to come? Certainly the references to the "princes

on the throne of David" should direct us to Christ, the great Son
of David, yet this by no means vitiates the importance of the Sabbath. The sober warning of Jeremiah to a Sabbath-breaking church
should grip our hearts as much today as it ought to have gripped
the hearts of the Israelites who first heard the prophet preach this
inspired and infallible Word from the Lord.

In Ezekiel 20, the prophet recounted the history of Israel's
rebellion as an indictment against them. In this chapter, there is a
repeated emphasis on the persistent Sabbath-breaking of God's people as a primary cause for His wrath upon them. To cite merely one
example, after recounting the blessings of bringing His people out
of Egypt and giving them His statutes and judgments, the Lord said,

> Moreover also I gave them my sabbaths, to be a sign between
> me and them, that they might know that I am the LORD that
> sanctify them. But the house of Israel rebelled against me
> in the wilderness: they walked not in my statutes, and they
> despised my judgments, which if a man do, he shall even live
> in them; and my sabbaths they greatly polluted: then I said, I
> would pour out my fury upon them in the wilderness, to con-
> sume them (vv. 12–13).

It is significant that on the four occasions in this chapter where
the Lord rebuked His people for breaking His statutes and judgments, the Sabbath is singled out from the rest of God's laws as a
particularly heinous sin. In fact, this sin along with idolatry are the
two most commonly cited causes of the exile in the prophetic books.
The Sabbath is often singled out as a particular blessing that God
gave to His people (see, for example, Neh. 9:14). If the Sabbath is a
special blessing and privilege given by God to His people, then it
should not be surprising that Sabbath-breaking draws the special
attention of the wrath of God.

In this connection, there is one matter of confusion with respect
to the New Testament teaching on the Sabbath that ought to be
addressed. Many assert that Jesus did not teach about the fourth
commandment in the same manner in which He treated the others.
Yet the Lord Jesus Christ addressed the subject of the Sabbath no

fewer than six times in the synoptic Gospels. You may still object (as many often do) that the manner in which He addressed the Sabbath was corrective only, whereas His teaching with respect to the other commandments included positive instructions. I cannot hope to examine the teaching of Jesus in detail in this short space, yet at least one often overlooked observation should be made. Although Jesus taught on the Sabbath in response to the abuses of the Pharisees, this is the *same manner* in which He dealt with all of the other commandments. The Sermon on the Mount, for example, should not be treated as Jesus' "new law" or as an expansion of the Ten Commandments. How many people have realized that much of the teaching of the Sermon on the Mount comes from Leviticus? The only commandment in the New Testament that is called "new" is Jesus' teaching that we are to love one another *as He has loved us* (John 13:34; 1 John 2:8–11). In light of this, it is not true to say that the Lord Jesus taught less about the Sabbath than the other commandments. He gave instructions concerning Sabbath-keeping more often than any other commandment. That He did so in a "negative" manner by contradicting the Pharisees does not reflect poorly upon the Sabbath, but rather upon the Pharisees.

The frequency with which the Sabbath appears in the law and the manner in which the prophets enforced it should cause the church to rouse herself out of slumber and seek to know the will of the Lord of the Sabbath with renewed earnestness. The prophets stand perpetually as God's prosecutors against His Sabbath-breaking people in every age. Should not the frequency with which the Sabbath is addressed in Scripture and the earnestness with which it is dealt serve to awaken us out of sleep?

The Sabbath and the Exile

The connection of Sabbath-breaking to Israel's exile highlights the importance of the Sabbath for the well-being of the church more than nearly any other factor. As early as Leviticus 26, the Lord began to warn the people of the consequences of breaking His covenant and promised that the eventual outcome of persistent rebellion would be exile. The Lord would execute "the quarrel of [His] covenant" (v. 25) and would make the land desolate by scattering His people among the nations (vv. 32–33). The same threat was repeated in Deuteronomy 4 and 32, with the prediction that the people of Israel would disobey the Lord and go into exile. It is well known that this occurred when God first sent the northern kingdom of Israel into the hands of the Assyrians, and later sent the southern kingdom of Judah into exile in Babylon under Nebuchadnezzar. Most of the canonical prophets of the Bible pressed the consciences of the people with the fact that God would not fail to fulfill the threats He had made in the Pentateuch. When the exile became inevitable, the prophet Jeremiah, by the inspiration of the Holy Spirit, pronounced that not only was the exile certain, but that it would last for seventy years (Jer. 25:11; 29:10; see Dan. 9). All of this is common knowledge to anyone who has read the Bible, since it occupies a large portion of the Old Testament. However, the role that Sabbath-breaking had to play in the exile of God's people is often overlooked.

Have you ever wondered why the Lord chose to exile Israel for exactly seventy years? The answer is connected to their Sabbath-breaking. After the Lord had promised that He would banish His people from the land for their sins, Leviticus 26:34–35 states: "Then shall the land enjoy her sabbaths, as long as it lieth desolate, and ye be in your enemies' land; even then shall the land rest, and enjoy her sabbaths. As long as it lieth desolate it shall rest [for the time it did not rest on your sabbaths when you dwelt in it]."[6] In accord with this warning, the duration of the exile was in proportion to duration of the time in which God's people had neglected His Sabbaths. It is noteworthy that the Sabbath was given special importance in relation to the covenant blessings and curses since, with the second commandment, it was inserted as a preface to these blessings and

---

6. The KJV does not present the idea underscored in the Hebrew to the effect that the land would remain desolate for the length of time that they had violated the Sabbath.

curses (vv. 1–2). In the preface to the covenant curses, as well as in the express words of these curses, the Sabbath was given a prominent place. When the exile came and Nebuchadnezzar destroyed Jerusalem and burned the temple, the author of 2 Chronicles wrote, "And them that had escaped the sword carried he away to Babylon; where they were servants to him and his sons until the reign of the kingdom of Persia: to fulfill the word of the LORD by the mouth of Jeremiah, until the land had enjoyed her sabbaths: for as long as she lay desolate she kept sabbath, to fulfill threescore and ten years" (36:20–21). Sabbath-breaking was not the only *reason* for the exile, but it was the sole factor that determined the *length* of the exile. In light of this fact, should not the widespread Sabbath-breaking of our day cause us great alarm?

Someone will object that the Sabbaths in view in these passages are not the weekly Sabbaths, but rather the Sabbaths of the seventh year in which the Lord commanded the people to give rest to the land. There is no doubt this was immediately in view in these passages. The Lord clearly speaks of the land resting by being emptied of its inhabitants, since the wicked inhabitants would not give the land rest while they lived there. It is, however, important to keep in mind that Israel had many "Sabbaths" (see Lev. 23), and that the summary principle enforcing all of them was the fourth commandment. The "Sabbath days," such as the seventh-year Sabbath, were aspects of the ceremonial law and would pass away with the coming of the new covenant in Christ (Col. 3:16). However, breaking the seventh-year Sabbath violated the principle of the fourth commandment. The primary emphasis of the fourth commandment is, as the Westminster Shorter Catechism states, "the keeping holy to God such set times as he hath appointed in his word" (Q. 58). This implies that we may keep holy to God *only* those days and times He appointed in His Word. For this reason, the same commandment requiring the seventh-year Sabbath, the Passover, the Day of Atonement, and so forth now expressly forbids observing them, since the Word of God no longer requires them. In a similar manner, the second commandment requires that God's people should worship Him only in those ways He has appointed. Thus the same commandment that required animal sacrifices in the Old Testament forbids them in the New Testament. The principles behind the Ten Commandments are unchangeable, even if God has changed the way some of them should be outwardly observed.

It should be clear that the primary significance of the passages cited above is not that Israel violated the seventh-year Sabbath, but that they violated the fourth commandment, which required this Sabbath. Should we assume that God's greatest concern in these passages was that the land had not been resting properly? Instead, should we not assume that the violation of the seventh-year Sabbath was a sign of contempt for the fourth commandment as a whole? The book of Nehemiah confirms this conclusion. In chapter 13, Nehemiah noted:

> In those days saw I in Judah some treading wine presses on the sabbath, and bringing in sheaves, and lading asses; as also wine, grapes, figs, and all manner of burdens, which they brought into Jerusalem on the sabbath day: and I testified against them in the day wherein they [were selling provisions]. There dwelt men of Tyre also therein, which brought fish, and [all kinds of goods], and sold on the sabbath unto the children of Judah, and in Jerusalem. Then I contended with the nobles of Judah, and said unto them, What evil thing is this that ye do, and profane the sabbath day? Did not your fathers thus, and did not our God bring all this [disaster] upon us, and upon this city? Yet ye bring more wrath upon Israel by profaning the sabbath (vv. 15–18).

That Nehemiah cited Sabbath-breaking as one of the primary causes of the wrath of God in the exile makes it difficult to conclude that he did not have in view passages such as Leviticus 26 and 2 Chronicles 36. Yet Nehemiah 13 reproved those violating the *weekly Sabbath*, not the seventh-year Sabbath. Neglecting the seventh-year Sabbath was only a symptom of the disease of a society that had complete disregard for the fourth commandment.

It is worth noting *how* the people in Nehemiah 13 broke the Sabbath. That they broke the Sabbath by working in their wine presses is obvious; however, two other factors are mentioned. First, they were "*selling* provisions" (v. 15), and second, they were *buying* provisions from people who were not part of the covenant community (vv. 16, 20). In chapter 10, the people had vowed explicitly that they would not do this very thing. They said, "If the peoples of the land brought wares or any grain to sell on the Sabbath day, we would not buy it from them on the Sabbath" (Neh. 10:31, my translation). In light of this broken vow, Nehemiah commanded the gates to be shut on the Sabbath, and he threatened to arrest the foreigners who returned the next week to continue their lucrative commerce on the Sabbath day (13:19, 21). The implications of this passage are obvious: we are not only commanded to refrain from our own labors on the Sabbath, but we must not *buy* and *sell* goods on the Sabbath. How does this apply to us today? It seems indisputable that we should not do grocery shopping on the Sabbath. It should also be shameful that so many Christians rush from corporate worship to restaurants on the Sabbath. Poor planning in not making sure we have enough gas in the car on Saturday does not make buying gas on Sunday a work of necessity; it is an act of sin that must be repented of by checking the gas gauge next Saturday.

Nehemiah severely rebuked the people for commerce on the Sabbath. How can we, in good conscience, pay someone else on the Sabbath to do that for which God once demanded the death penalty? Though we should not apply this penalty today, do we dare say that God chose a punishment out of proportion to the crime? How can we pay someone to perform a task that would be sin for us to perform? The reasoning of believers at this point is, frankly, appalling. Many argue that it is lawful for them to take advantage of the labor of others on the Sabbath since they will work with or without our patronage. Does this type of reasoning give me the right to knowingly buy stolen property with impunity, under the pretence that the person was going to sell it anyway? What of those who argue that non-Christian restaurant servers and grocery store cashiers do not acknowledge the Sabbath, and therefore it is lawful for us to pay for their services on the Sabbath? Were the men of Tyre at the gates of Jerusalem Israelites who knew the law? Did Nehemiah excuse Israel for trading with them because they were unbelieving foreigners? My challenge to those who deny the *principle* that the Sabbath forbids us from supporting the unlawful labors of others is that if the warning given in Nehemiah 13 should not be applied in this manner, how is this passage applicable at all? How then is this passage profitable for reproof and instruction in righteousness (2 Tim. 3:16)? The lowest common denominator of Sabbath-keeping should include the *principle* that we should not work on the day and that we should not cause others to work, with the exception of cases of necessity and mercy.[7]

If Sabbath-breaking is cited as a cause for sending Israel into exile, how long will God patiently observe our disregard for His day before severely chastening our sins? Sabbath-breaking is one of the best ways to ensure the devastation of our churches and of our nation, just as it was for Israel. By her Sabbath-breaking, is the

---

7. I have highlighted the word, "principle" because it is precisely at this point that I will be accused of attempting to set up a so-called list of "do's" and "don'ts." The proposition that we must not cause others to work on the Sabbath is not a list of particulars, but a principle that must be applied to particular situations. Principles must be applied. This is why I have tried to give some examples that ought to be clear and less debatable. A more difficult example would be whether or not using public transportation on the Lord's Day in order to go to church is a work of necessity. John Murray, who was known as a "strict" Sabbatarian, was unfortunately barred from licensure in his home church in Scotland for allowing freedom of conscience over this issue. See Iain Murray, *The Life of John Murray*, in *The Collected Writings of John Murray* (Edinburgh: Banner of Truth, 1982), 3:35–36. In debates over applying our principles, there will always be disputes to a greater or lesser degree, and sadly some will always lean toward an extrabiblical pharisaism. Yet where the modern church has failed at this point is that she has lost the *principles* of Sabbath-keeping, such as the one drawn from Nehemiah 13. If we are honest with ourselves, our only practical attempt at Sabbath-keeping is often not going to work on that day—at least some of the time. For more on principles, see chapter 4.

church prompting God to send her into a new "Babylonian captivity"? Or has her captivity already begun? Surely Joseph Pipa was correct when he asked, "Is it not possible that one reason for the spiritual weakness of the church is her failure to honor God on the Lord's Day?"[8]

8. Pipa, *The Lord's Day*, 13.

CHAPTER TWO

The Importance of
God's Day of Worship

In Ezekiel 8, the Lord revealed the horrors of Israel's idolatry. In each part of the vision, the Lord showed the prophet some form of idolatry that was being committed in the temple of God itself. Yet the Lord acknowledged degrees of the sin of idolatry. In each successive stage of the vision, He told Ezekiel, "Turn thee yet again, and thou shalt see greater abominations" (vv. 6, 13, 15). This has often been referred to as Ezekiel's "chamber of imagery."[1] In a similar fashion, the previous chapter highlighted the importance of the Sabbath in the eyes of our Lord in a progressive manner. The violation of a creation ordinance is a high crime, while neglecting a sign of the covenant of grace is a greater abomination. The frequency with which the Scriptures enforce the fourth commandment adds to the seriousness of the issue. The fact that Sabbath-breaking was singled out as one of the most significant causes of the exile of God's people raises the significance of the issue to a new height. Yet as we come to consider the glory of the Sabbath as a day designed exclusively for worship and communion with God, Sabbath-breaking is set forth in all its blackness as base ingratitude. Therefore, turn aside and I will show you "greater abominations" than these.

The crux of the debate over what is lawful on the Sabbath is if the purpose of the day is *rest* or of "spending the entire time in the public and private exercises of God's *worship*" (Shorter Catechism,

---

1. For example, John Owen and Thomas Peck both appropriated this language to describe the Roman Catholic Church.

Q. 60). The manner in which you answer this question determines how you will seek to observe the day. This point determines how you will answer every question respecting what thoughts, words, and works are appropriate on the Sabbath, as well as whether or not worldly recreations that are lawful on other days are also lawful on the Sabbath. If you believe that the purpose of the day is *rest*, then the emphasis of your Sabbath-keeping will be upon what makes you feel most rested. Conversely, if you believe the purpose of the Sabbath is setting the day apart for corporate, private, and family *worship*, you will exclude all practices that are inconsistent with or do not immediately promote worship. I will address this matter again in chapters 4 and 6, and I will seek to come to the same conclusions from slightly different approaches. Four initial reasons the emphasis of the Sabbath day is rest from our regular employments for the purpose of worship and communion with God are inferred from the situation of Adam and Eve in the garden of Eden; the fact that God "sanctified" the Sabbath; the position of the Sabbath within the Ten Commandments; and the character of the duties associated with Sabbath-keeping.

The Garden of Eden

First, the situation in the garden of Eden implies that God designed the Sabbath for worship and communion with Himself. God sanctified the Sabbath as soon as the sixth day of creation was completed (Gen. 2:1–3). The Ten Commandments remind us that this example set by God constituted the pattern to be followed by mankind. The Sabbath was given to Adam and Eve prior to the Fall. It initially had no regard either to sin or to redemption. It was not given as a type of Christ as the Redeemer, since there was no sin and death from which to be redeemed, and it was not given as a type of salvation, which was irrelevant to an unfallen man and woman. In the garden, Adam and Eve lived every day in worship and service to God. Part of their joyful service was the labor God had given them. On the day on which God called them to imitate Him in His own rest, they had no activity left other than direct acts of communion with God. What more could a sinless man and woman desire? What other purpose could the Sabbath have served in Paradise?

The "rest" required on the Sabbath cannot be equated with inactivity; it was not so with God Himself, who has never ceased to labor in His works of providence (John 5:17), and neither should it be in the case of His creatures as they imitate His rest. Robert L. Reymond has observed that "'rest' cannot mean mere cessation from labor, much less recovery from fatigue.... 'Rest' then means involvement in *new,* in the sense of *different,* activity. It means cessation of the labor of the six days and the taking up of different labors appropriate to the Lord's Day. What these labors of the Sabbath rest are is circumscribed by the accompanying phrase, 'to the Lord.' They certainly include both corporate and private acts of worship and the contemplation of the glory of God."[2] We must also avoid the error of concluding that since we must live all of life to the glory of God (Rom. 12:1–2; 1 Cor. 10:31), we may worship God on the Sabbath in every activity in which we may serve him on other days. John Murray exposed the absurdity of this position: "While it is true that we ought to serve the Lord every day and in all things we must not forget that there are different ways of serving God. We do not serve him by doing the same thing all the time. If we do that, we are either insane or notoriously perverse. There is a great variety in human vocation. If we neglect to observe that variation, we shall soon pay the cost."[3] This is patently obvious from the fact that although we

---

2. Robert L. Reymond, "Lord's Day Observance," in *Contending for the Faith: Lines in the Sand That Strengthen the Church* (Fearn, U.K.: Christian Focus Publications, 2005), 181.

3. John Murray, "The Sabbath Institution," in *Collected Writings,* 1:209 (emphasis original). The Puritan David Dickson, in emphasizing the point that the Sabbath cannot be kept merely by specific acts of worship on the day but by dedicating the entire day for worship, added the interesting point that if all that was required was to "set apart some indefinite time" on the day for worship, then the Sabbath would not differ substantially from the other days of the week on which worship was required as well. David Dickson, *Truth's Victory over Error: A Commentary on the Westminster Confession of Faith*

must labor for six days to the glory of God (Col. 3:23), this act of "worship" is forbidden on the Sabbath day.

Surely Adam and Eve would have enjoyed the Sabbath according to its original intent: as a day of uninterrupted and direct worship and communion with God. For this reason, Murray added:

> There is release from the labors of the six days, but it is also release to the contemplation of the glory of God. Cessation from the labors of the week must itself have its source and ground in obedience to God, and the gratitude which is the motive and fruit of such obedience will minister to the worship which is the specific employment of the Sabbath rest. This is just saying that rest from weekly labors and the exercises of specific worship are inseparable and they mutually condition one another. It is a Sabbath of rest *to the Lord;* we cannot have the one without the other.[4]

The purpose of the Sabbath is not inactivity. This was essentially the view of the Pharisees. The purpose of cessation from worldly employments on the Sabbath is to take up the *entire* time with the public and private exercises of God's worship. For this reason Murray concluded: "Even in innocence man would have required time for specific worship. We are too ready to entertain the notion that religion in a state of sinless confirmed integrity would have required no institutions as the medium of expression.... Unfallen man would need to suspend his weekly labors in order to refresh himself with the exercises of concentrated worship."[5]

(1684; reprint, Edinburgh: Banner of Truth, 2007), 155. If the fourth commandment requires worship at all, it requires worship as the emphasis of the entire day. If the fourth commandment requires rest only, then the worship required on the Sabbath is no different from that required every other day.

4. Murray, "Sabbath Institution," 210 (emphasis original).

5. Murray, *Principles of Conduct*, 34.

God "Sanctified" the Sabbath

Second, the fact that the Lord "sanctified" or "hallowed" the Sabbath day means that He set it apart for the purposes of worship.[6] Leviticus 27 addresses the subject of people, animals, various objects, and offerings that were dedicated as holy to the Lord. These people and objects were dedicated to the service of the tabernacle and were of use in the worship and service of the Lord. Objects that were holy to the Lord belonged to the Lord in a peculiar manner. The Lord said, "No devoted thing, that a man shall devote unto the LORD of all that he hath, both of man and beast, and of the field of his possession, shall be sold or redeemed: every devoted thing is most holy unto the LORD" (Lev. 27:28). So when God sanctified the Sabbath and made it "holy," the natural conclusion is that He set it apart for worship. In every case, whether an object is declared holy, devoted to the Lord, or sanctified, the emphasis always rests upon setting something apart *exclusively* to the service of the Lord. This means that the operative phrase in the fourth commandment is "Keep it holy," not "You shall do no work."[7]

The Position among the Ten Commandments

Third, the position of the fourth commandment among the Ten Commandments points to an emphasis upon worship. The first four commandments are generally acknowledged to address our direct relation to God with respect to His worship and service, while the last six address our service to God by way of serving our neighbor. The first commandment concerns the object of worship, the second the manner of worship, the third the proper attitude of worship, and the fourth the time set apart exclusively for worship.[8] The grossest

---

6. For a more in-depth examination of this point, see Campbell, *On the First Day of the Week: God, the Christian, and the Sabbath*, 45–48. Also see Pipa, *Lord's Day*, 32–34. This point will be readdressed in chapter 4.

7. See my "Five Reasons Why the Sabbath Is Designed for Worship," *Puritan Reformed Journal* 1, no. 2 (2009): 218–25.

8. John Owen added that the fourth commandment is "the keeper of the whole first table," since it is designed to ensure that the worship required by

evidence I have encountered that the church has moved away from understanding the Sabbath as a day of worship was a sermon on the fourth commandment entitled, "Take a Rest. You Deserve It." The Sabbath was made for man and not man for the Sabbath (Mark 2:27), yet many contemporary Christians have abused this principle in order to shift from a worship-centered view of the Sabbath to a man-centered view of the Sabbath.

The Duties of the Sabbath

Fourth, every duty explicitly connected to Sabbath observance is a duty related to worship. Every Sabbath, Israel must hold a "holy convocation" to the Lord (Lev. 23:3). The morning and evening sacrifices, which were an integral part of temple worship, must be doubled on the Sabbath. Psalm 92, titled "A Psalm for the Sabbath Day," depicts God's people giving thanks to the Most High and praising His name morning and evening, with instruments and gladness for making His people triumph through the works of His hands (Ps. 92:1–4). In the New Testament, the disciples gathered together as a body on the first day of the week as Paul preached to them (Acts 20:7ff). The first day of the week, or the Lord's Day, was singled out as the most appropriate time for taking an offering for the poor (1 Cor. 16:1–2). In short, every requirement attached to Sabbath-keeping in both the Old and New Testaments relates to some duty of corporate or private worship. If you consider these commands in isolation, you may be tempted to conclude that the Sabbath is a day of rest with duties of worship attached to it. However, when you connect the character of these commands with the four inferences drawn above, you must conclude that the Sabbath is a day of worship in which rest from your weekly employments is a necessary *prerequisite*. The

the first three commandments is properly observed. John Owen, "A Day of Sacred Rest," in *An Exposition to the Epistle to the Hebrews* (n.d.; repr., Edinburgh: Banner of Truth, 1991), 2:289.

presumption is that worship is the reason for which the entire day was set apart by the Lord for Himself.[9]

This evidence shows that God appointed the Sabbath day for us to rest from our worldly employments so we might have a day of worship and communion with God. When our sole focus on that day is upon worshiping and communing with our God through the glorious gospel of His Son, practical questions regarding our thoughts, speech, and recreations on that day will begin to answer themselves. As the Scottish theologian John Dick pointed out, "He who understands in what the sanctification of the Sabbath consists, has no need that the sins in the fourth commandment should be pointed out to him."[10] This slightly overstates the case, but it illustrates the point that most disagreements over Sabbath-keeping result from a lack of clarity regarding how to sanctify the day. What a glorious privilege and blessing such a day ought to be to us! What a mercy from God that we should have one day in seven to enjoy God without the distractions encumbering us throughout the week! Does this not make our neglect of the Sabbath appear as base ingratitude? If Adam and Eve needed a day of worship before the Fall, do you not need such a day? When you disregard the Sabbath by bending your conscience to the will of employers or to the lusts of the flesh rather than to the Word of God, do you realize you are actually despising the privilege of worship? You are not simply disobeying a commandment of God; you are spurning one of His greatest gifts to mankind. The fact that the Sabbath is designed to be a day of worship and communion with God brings us deep into this "chamber of imagery." Does not this highlight the importance of the Sabbath more than every other factor combined?

---

9. For more on this point, see Reymond, "Lord's Day Observance,"180.

10. John Dick, *Lectures on Theology* (Edinburgh: Oliver & Boyd, 1838; repr., Stoke on Trent, U.K.: Tentmaker Publications, 2004), 4:459.

Conclusions

A few controversial details of Sabbath-keeping have already been set forth here. Each of these will be addressed more fully in subsequent chapters. However, all who believe that the Sabbath is a perpetually binding commandment will agree that as a minimum, our weekly employments are forbidden. Yet what if your employer desires you to work on the Sabbath just one time? Excluding works of necessity (such as firemen, police, doctors, nurses, and so forth),[11] have you considered the seriousness of the situation? Consider that your sin does not affect yourself alone, but the entire church. The sin of one Achan brought defeat to the entire army (Josh. 7). One Sabbath breaker brought guilt on the entire nation if his sin was not dealt with properly (Num. 15:32–36; read in light of vv. 30–31). One act of Saul against the Gibeonites brought the chastening hand of the Lord against Israel under the reign of David (2 Sam. 21). One man living in an adulterous relationship brought shame upon the entire church (1 Cor. 5). We are too ready to sin when the world pressures us to do so, simply because we fear conflict. Does this not betray the fact that in reality we fear him who can harm the body more than Him who casts both body and soul into hell? It seems harmless to lay a command of God aside *just once* for the sake of convenience and comfort. At the heart of this, however, is an exaltation of our own comfort above the authority of God and His Word. Though of a far lesser nature, it has the same root as apostasy.

---

11. In accord with the example and teaching of Jesus, I am assuming that what have typically been called works of "necessity" and works of "mercy" are lawful on the Sabbath day. John Dick has provided helpful definitions of these: "By the former, are meant works which could not have been done on the preceding day, and cannot be deferred to the next.... Works of mercy are those which are performed from compassion to our fellow creatures." Dick, 4:460. Timothy Dwight has added a useful caution that will prevent the abuse of works of necessity and mercy in order to justify our own ways on the Sabbath: "All works, both of necessity and mercy, are to be regarded as Duties, which we are bound to perform; and never as indulgences, which we are permitted to take." *Theology Explained and Defended* (New York: Harper & Brothers, 1850; repr., Birmingham: Solid Ground Christian Books, 2005), 3:267–68.

What if refusing to work on the Sabbath even one time brings the risk of losing employment? After all, must not a man provide for his family? God already anticipated this objection and answered it with a bare assertion of His authority. He said, "Six days thou shalt work, but on the seventh day thou shalt rest: in earing time and in harvest thou shalt rest" (Ex. 34:21). Even if the crops were ripe for the harvest and the farmer did not know what weather would come tomorrow, he must still keep the Sabbath.[12] You plead the harm that might come to your family if you refuse to work on God's holy day. Should you not more greatly fear the harm that God has promised will come to your family, your church, and your nation if you agree to do so? Is it not true that the principle by which many of us operate is that as long as we do not *volunteer* to work on the Sabbath, we dutifully keep the commandment? We must beware that we do not act as though our employers sovereignly provide for our families rather than God. The martyrs chose to face death rather than sin against God. The Puritan Jeremiah Burroughs made the astute observation that although not every Christian will be called to martyrdom, every Christian must be a potential martyr.[13] Repercussions at work, though difficult, are a much *easier* opportunity to suffer joyfully for the sake of obedience to Christ than torture or

---

12. "Work during the plowing and harvest times was prohibited on the Sabbath (Ex. 34:21), presumably because people claimed that the limited period available to complete these tasks justified ignoring the Sabbath." Rowland S. Ward, "The Lord's Day and the Westminster Confession," in *The Faith Once Delivered* (Phillipsburg, N.J.: P&R, 2007), 198. John Owen dismissed the continuing application of this verse on the grounds that it represented harsh regulations that were a part of the Jewish economy. Owen, *Hebrews*, 2:401–2. However, this is a strange anomaly, since in the same context Owen argued that even the Jewish judicial laws consisted of the application of the moral law. Presumably, Owen was concerned about the apparent contradiction between the prohibition contained in this passage and the provision of Christ for works of necessity on the Sabbath. There is no contradiction, however, since the person envisioned in Exodus 34:21 would have likely justified working every Sabbath during plowing time and harvest under the pretence of necessity.

13. Jeremiah Burroughs, *The Saints Happiness: 41 Sermons on the Beatitudes* (1660; repr., Morgan, Pa.: Soli Deo Gloria, 1996), 203–4.

death. Perhaps the reason Christians have suffered so little persecu-
tion in the United States is that Satan has already gained victory by
convincing us that it is better to obey men rather than God. The
Sabbath is one indicator among many that this is the case.

Disobedience never has, and never will be, an acceptable means
of delivering ourselves from trouble. It is perhaps the ultimate denial
of the sovereignty of God (Heb. 13:5–6 provides the remedy). Do we
ultimately have control over earning an income and providing for
our families? Do we not believe that it is more costly to disobey God
than to suffer at the hands of our employers? Do we not believe that
God is sovereign over our employers and has ordained the situations
in which they test our obedience to Him? For this reason, Heinrich
Bullinger wrote, "They therefore do err from the truth as far as the
heaven is wide, whosoever despise the religion and holy rest of the
Sabbath-day…and do labor on the Sabbath-day, as they do on working days, under the pretence of care for their family and necessity's
sake."[14] My dear reader, refusing to work on the Sabbath is Sabbath-
keeping in its *easiest* form. If we refuse to be faithful in the least of
these matters, how then will we be faithful with greater things?

I know that in a time when the Sabbath is despised by the church
as well as the world, these sayings are extraordinarily difficult, but
the alternative is even more difficult. We must make the choice either
to offend God or to offend men by our humble obedience to God. The
church has underestimated the importance of Sabbath-keeping and
the threats of God against Sabbath-breaking. Unless the passages
cited above no longer bear the weight of the authority of God upon
the church as His infallible and immutable will, then the widespread
disregard of the Sabbath is like a cancer that is eating the heart out
of the church. The first act of grace and love toward us on the part
of God is to sound the alarm against our sins. Our Great Physi-
cian often wounds before He heals. Yet He is a God who delights in

---

14. Henry Bullinger, *The Decades of Henry Bullinger*, ed. Thomas Harding
(Parker Society 1849–1852; repr., Grand Rapids: Reformation Heritage Books,
2004), 1:259.

showing mercy (Mic. 7:18). The call of God to His Sabbath-breaking church is: "Draw nigh to God, and he will draw nigh to you. Cleanse your hands, ye sinners; and purify your hearts, ye double-minded. Be afflicted [lament], and mourn, and weep: let your laughter be turned to mourning, and your joy to heaviness. Humble yourselves in the sight of the Lord, and he shall lift you up" (James 4:8–10).

Although this chapter has emphasized threats and warnings, I urge you to keep two things in view: the threats and warnings are from God; and they are part of His Fatherly love in causing His people to see the horrors of sin and the glories of His mercies in Christ. Our Father in heaven chastens those whom He loves, and often the chastening love of a father begins with a rebuke from his mouth. "If ye endure chastening, God dealeth with you as with sons; for what son is he whom the father chasteneth not?" (Heb. 12:7).

Disagreements over Sabbath-keeping should not rupture the fellowship of believers, and the doctrine of the Sabbath does not share the importance of the doctrine of justification or the authority of Scripture. Yet neither do the Scriptures treat the Sabbath as a peripheral issue. Can we honestly say that the modern church has attached the same importance to Sabbath-keeping that God has? Whatever position you adopt with respect to Sabbath-keeping, may the weight the Word of God attaches to this subject drive you to study these things with greater urgency and with increased earnestness to understand the will of the Lord.

CHAPTER THREE

The Presuppositions of
Isaiah 58:13–14

A breakdown in communication is difficult to overcome. You have probably heard a discussion between two people described as "getting their lines crossed." We all know the agonizing experience of debating an issue and speaking past rather than to one another. This often occurs when two people discuss what God has required in order to keep the Sabbath day holy. It is one thing to understand the importance of the Sabbath; it is another thing to understand what Sabbath-keeping means. Most discussions about Sabbath-keeping tend to revolve around the proper interpretation of Isaiah 58:13–14, which may justifiably be called the *locus classicus* for questions regarding Sabbath-keeping asked since at least the end of the sixteenth century. Differences over this passage, however, often result from our being unaware of the presuppositions we bring to it. Confusion occurs and progress is stinted when one or both parties are unaware of their own presuppositions or those of the other person. As a result, it is extraordinarily difficult, if not impossible, for one side to convince the other. Sadly, we end up sounding like children with one side asserting, "This is what the text means," and the other saying more vehemently, "No it doesn't!"

Two arguments are generally leveled against the "Puritan" view of the Sabbath. The first is that the picture of Sabbath-keeping presented in the Westminster Standards is based upon a doubtful understanding of Isaiah 58:13–14, and the second is that it rests almost exclusively upon this same passage.

I will address the first of these arguments. The primary area of disagreement over this passage is whether or not "worldly recreations" as well as "worldly employments" are forbidden on the Sabbath day. In this chapter and the next, I hope to convince you that our presuppositions regarding the nature and purpose of the Sabbath day determine, limit, and direct our reading of Isaiah 58:13–14.[1] The presupposition that the *entire* Sabbath day has been sanctified by God for Himself as a day for public and private worship leads to the conclusion that "the Sabbath is to be sanctified by a holy resting all that day, even from such worldly employments and recreations as are lawful on other days; and spending the whole time in the public and private exercises of God's worship" (Shorter Catechism, Q. 60).[2] My purpose is not to repeat the sound exposition of this passage provided by other authors. I hope to demonstrate why we often disagree over this passage and cause us to reexamine the importance of the presuppositions we bring to it. I will begin by tracing the presuppositions Isaiah brought to the passage, offer a brief exposition of the commands and prohibitions of the text,

---

1. With his typical astuteness, John Owen recognized that whether or not the whole day should be set apart "for the solemn worship of God," both corporately and privately, was the key factor in determining all questions relating to Sabbath-keeping. "Indeed, herein lies secretly...the principal cause of all the strife that has been and is in the world about this matter. Men may teach the doctrine of a sabbatical rest on what principles they please, deduce it from what original they think good, if they plead not for an *exactness of duty* in its observance, if they bind not a *religious, careful attendance* on the worship of God, in public and private, on the consciences of other men, if they require not a watchfulness against all diversions and avocations from the duties of the day, they may do it without much fear of opposition; for all the concernments of doctrines and opinions which tend unto practice are regulated thereby, and embraced or rejected as the practice pleaseth or displeaseth that they lead unto." Owen, "Day of Sacred Rest," 271 (emphasis original). In other words, if men are not governed by the notion that the entire day is set apart for public and private worship, practically speaking, they will end up doing as they please on the day. Note that Owen would have included "recreations" under "diversions."

2. For the remainder of Q. 60 regarding works of necessity and mercy, see below.

answer some significant objections that have not been addressed adequately, and explore briefly the glorious promises attached to Sabbath-keeping. In light of these promises, we will see that by neglecting the Sabbath the church has been depriving herself of some of the greatest blessings in all of Scripture.

The Significance of the Context

We are not the only ones who bring previously held ideas and convictions into a discussion; the authors of Scripture brought the presuppositions of earlier biblical revelation to bear on their inspired writings. For this reason, it is scarcely possible to evaluate the nature of the events in the books of Samuel, Kings, and Chronicles without some familiarity with the books of Moses. Israel's prophets also presupposed the significance of the covenant with Abraham, Isaac, and Jacob, as well as the importance of the Mosaic Law, when they used these truths to enforce the warnings and promises they preached. They did not construct a theology concerning these things, but rather *assumed* one that was already in place. The prophets often clarified and expanded these subjects, but they did not lay the foundation for them a second time. This means that the prophets often presupposed a theological and historical framework that both undergirded and gave weight to their messages.

For this reason, the teaching of the prophets on the purpose of the Sabbath is indirect. It can be understood properly only in light of the teaching and implications of earlier books of the Bible. The surrounding context of Isaiah 58 hints that Isaiah assumed that the Sabbath ought to be a day set apart to God for the purposes of worship. There are at least two observations regarding the context of Isaiah that bear this out. The first is that the references to the Sabbath in chapters 56 and 66 demonstrate that Sabbath-keeping is intimately tied to *acts of worship* under the new covenant. The second is the attempt to unravel the question of the relationship between the Sabbath and fasting in the chapter itself. These considerations will help you begin to appreciate how the theological baggage you bring to Isaiah 58:13–14 determines your reading of the passage. The assumptions implied in Isaiah's teaching about the Sabbath reinforce the inference that the Sabbath was meant to be a day of rest sanctified for the purposes of worship.

The Broad Context

What I have to say about the Sabbath in the book of Isaiah is not new, nor is it even a significant contribution. You may find excellent treatments of the relation of Sabbath-keeping to the new covenant in Isaiah, for example, in Joseph Pipa's book on the Lord's Day and Alec Motyer's commentary on Isaiah.[3] It is vital to understand that the relevant passages in chapters 56 and 66 demonstrate the integral place of the Sabbath under new covenant worship. However, it is easy to overlook the simple fact that these passages *assume* that the significance of the Sabbath is found in its connection to worship.

In chapter 56, the Sabbath is mentioned three times. Sabbath-keeping is singled out here as *the* primary characteristic of the person who "keeps judgment" and "does justice" (v. 1). In rapid succession, the Lord asserted, "Blessed is the man that doeth this, and the son of man that layeth hold on it: that keepeth the sabbath from polluting it, and keepeth his hand from doing any evil.… For thus saith the LORD unto the eunuchs that keep my sabbaths, and choose the things that please me, and take hold of my covenant.… Also the sons of the stranger, that join themselves to the LORD, to serve him, and to love the name of the LORD, to be his servants, every one that keepeth the Sabbath from polluting it, and taketh hold of my covenant" (vv. 2, 4, 6).[4] In the overall context, the Lord had promised the coming of his Suffering Servant (the Lord Jesus Christ), who would be wounded for the transgressions of His people, make His soul an offering for their sins, and be given as a covenant for the salvation of the nations

---

3. Pipa, *Lord's Day*, 15–16; J. Alec Motyer, *The Prophecy of Isaiah: An Introduction & Commentary* (Downers Grove, Ill.: InterVarsity, 1993), 459–67, 478–84.

4. Note the implicit connection between keeping the Sabbath and keeping the covenant. This is reminiscent of passages such as Exodus 31.

(53:5, 10; 42:6). As Pipa wrote, "This entire section of Isaiah refers ultimately to Jesus Christ and the New Covenant people."[5]

The two groups called to join themselves to the people of the Lord are "the son of the stranger" and "the eunuch" (v. 3). These people would be given a place and a name in God's holy temple better than that of sons and daughters (v. 5). They would come to God's "house of prayer for all people," and there offer prayer and burnt offerings (v. 7). Although Isaiah used the language of Old Testament worship, neither foreigners nor eunuchs were allowed to participate in corporate worship under the old covenant (see Lev. 21:20; Deut. 23:1; Ezek. 44:9). Isaiah was looking forward to the time when the floodgates of mercy would be opened, and the grace of God would flow freely to all peoples and in every nation. Eunuchs would be saved and called by the name of the Lord (Acts 8:27, 38–40), and Gentiles and Jews would be saved through the same faith in Jesus Christ (Acts 15:11).[6] It is significant that in singling out Sabbath-keeping as a sign of faithfulness to the covenant, Isaiah immediately drew attention to attending corporate worship. Worship was the primary activity attached to the Sabbath in the law, and Isaiah pointed to attendance at corporate worship as evidence of faithful Sabbath-keeping. Worship is not treated as a duty to be performed on the Sabbath, but worship is treated as integral to the concept of Sabbath-keeping.

In Isaiah 66:22–24, the Sabbath appears among the closing words of the book. The immediate context, which is the climactic moment of Isaiah's prophecy, depicts the gathering of the nations to come to see the glory of the Lord (v. 18). Some from among these nations would become the "brethren" of God's people (v. 20), and God promised to "take some of them for priests and Levites" (v. 21). Surely it is under the new covenant in Christ that Gentiles would receive such tremendous blessings! After promising to perpetuate the name and descendents of these people as long as the new

---

5. Pipa, *Lord's Day*, 15.

6. See Allan Harman, *Isaiah: A Covenant to Be Kept for the Sake of the Church* (Fearn, U.K.: Christian Focus Publications, 2005), 377–79.

heavens and new earth should last (v. 22; compare with the "place" and "name" given to foreigners and eunuchs in 56:5), Isaiah said, "And it shall come to pass, that from one new moon to another, and from one sabbath to another, all flesh shall come to worship before me, saith the LORD" (v. 23). However you understand the details of this passage, the Sabbath is clearly connected with the new covenant.[7] It is noteworthy to connect the Sabbath with corporate worship. The "new moon" was one of the days set apart for worship and thanksgiving under the Old Covenant. Although the "new moon" feasts should not be observed now (Col. 2:16), the primary activity Isaiah attached both to it, and to the Sabbath day, was worshiping in the presence of God.

Notice the close relationship between the Sabbath and worship in these passages. What were the eunuchs and foreigners doing on the Sabbath? They were coming to the temple for corporate worship. What were the people in chapter 66 doing from Sabbath to Sabbath? All flesh was coming to worship the Lord. It is significant that Isaiah assumed that the Sabbath was designed for worship and that his readers would understand why attending the place of corporate worship on the Sabbath was a sign of faithful Sabbath-keeping. Isaiah is like a professor teaching a course in which he assumes his students have taken other courses that are prerequisite to his instruction. In the Old Testament, whether the people were able to attend worship at the temple every Sabbath or not, they were commanded to have a "holy convocation" every Sabbath (Lev. 23:3). The Sabbath was "sanctified" by God (Gen. 2:2–3) to be holy for His worship and service. These passages in Isaiah are consistent with the assertion that the whole day should be "holy to the Lord" and set apart exclusively for worship. Isaiah did not commend people for resting on the Sabbath day, but he did commend them for worshiping on the Sabbath day. If Isaiah, under divine inspiration, believed that resting from

---

7. For a thorough and interesting exposition of this passage and its implications for the perpetuity of the Sabbath, see Campbell, *On the First Day of the Week*, 84–85.

labor was the dominant feature of Sabbath-keeping, is it not strange
that the only activity he attached to Sabbath- keeping was worship?
As Adam and Eve rested from the joys of labor in Paradise on one
day in seven in order to turn exclusively to the greater joys of uninterrupted worship and communion with God, so the foreigners and
eunuchs in Isaiah 56 and 66 demonstrated their faithfulness to God
by gathering together for worship on the Sabbath day. It is vital to
bear this in mind when we come to 58:13–14.

The Immediate Context

As you read Isaiah 58, have you ever wondered why two verses
regarding Sabbath-keeping appear almost abruptly at the close of a
discussion about fasting? The arguments of the book of Isaiah ordinarily flow through the course of many chapters in one continuous
stream of thought. For example, chapters 13–24 seamlessly address
the judgment of God upon several of the most prominent nations
of the world, with chapter 24 summarizing the whole by describ-
ing the earth, after the devastation of its nations, as "empty" and
"waste" (24:1). Chapters 40–46 contain an extended and carefully
argued polemic against idolatry, and there are many other examples.
To treat Isaiah as though anything in his prophecy was thrown in
"at random" would be like treating the apostle Paul as though his
discussion of sanctification and personal godliness in the book of
Romans "randomly" followed his discussion of justification by faith
alone in Christ alone.[8]

If this is true, what is the rational connection between fasting
and the Sabbath in Isaiah 58? We have already seen how Sabbath-
keeping relates to the broader topic of the coming of the new
covenant in Christ, yet why should the Sabbath be reintroduced at

---

8. That the entire prophecy of Isaiah reads so smoothly from beginning
to end as one coherent and unbroken argument makes it strange, in my mind,
that anyone would think the book is a compilation of multiple authors. The
places where these imaginary authors are identified are often the places where
Isaiah's argument is progressing to the next stage and he is altering his subject
matter accordingly.

this juncture in particular? After God's free offer of mercy in chapter 55, His exhortation and promises to all people in chapter 56, and His call and encouragement to repentance in chapter 57, Isaiah began "answering objections" in chapter 58. In verse 1, God commanded the prophet: "Cry aloud, spare not, lift up thy voice like a trumpet, and shew my people their transgression, and the house of Jacob their sins." Verses 2–3 essentially record the objection of the people to God's accusation against them. They pleaded as people who had not forgotten the ways and ordinances of the Lord, and they professed surprise at the fact that God had not heard them.

The Lord responded by first addressing the subject they had introduced, which was their fasting. God demonstrated what was inherently wrong with their fasting, taught them what kind of fasting pleased Him, and then implied that their emphasis upon fasting as a primary sign of piety was misplaced. They were using fasting as an opportunity to boast in their own religious achievements (vv. 2, 5). While they did so, they displayed religious hypocrisy by committing injustice, by oppressing their laborers (v. 3), by indulging in violence (v. 4), and by neglecting the poor (vv. 6–7). The Lord called them to repentance: first, by teaching them how to fast properly and to repent of the injustices they were guilty of; and second, by showing them a more excellent way of obedience and service, by means of Sabbath-keeping. As we saw in chapter 1, the Sabbath is treated as a "litmus test" of the spiritual condition of God's people. On the one hand, the connection between fasting and the Sabbath in this chapter seems to be that while fasting was always a subsidiary part of service to the Lord, Sabbath-keeping was absolutely vital and central. God regulated fasting, but man determined the occasions and frequency of fasting as each situation required. On the other hand, the Sabbath was a frequently recurring day dedicated to the worship and service of God. It is a continuing plague among men to emphasize duties that are less important in the eyes of God, while neglecting those that strike at the heart of biblical religion. The people had degenerated to a man-centered form of "religious" fasting; Sabbath-keeping was presented as the remedy to their problem because of its unquestionably God-centered nature. Ironically, while Israel was pointing to their days of fasting and mourning, God was directing them to His day of feasting and rejoicing. Nothing kills worldliness, pride, and formality in religion like devoting one whole day of every week to worship and communion with God.

There is, however, probably an additional connection between the Sabbath and fasting. In speaking to numerous people about this passage over a decade or so, I am increasingly convinced that many disagreements over verses 13–14 stem from how we understand the relationship between fasting and the Sabbath in this chapter. One reason why we speak past one another is that we have all adopted a viewpoint regarding this relationship that rarely comes explicitly into our discussions. At this stage, the opposing assumptions we bring to the passage begin to clash. What frequently occurs is that one group of people assumes or implies that the instructions concerning fasting determine the parameters for the discussion of Sabbath-keeping at the end of the chapter. The other group of people appeals to the broader context, makes reference to Isaiah 56 and 66, and expounds 58:13–14 while virtually ignoring verses 1–12. I suggest a third option: instead of viewing the instructions concerning fasting as the pattern for Sabbath-keeping, or ignoring them entirely, perhaps the connection between the two might be that Sabbath-keeping, in some sense, is the pattern for fasting.[9]

Many comparisons can be made between Sabbath-keeping and fasting. Although the Sabbath is a part of the Ten Commandments and must be observed weekly, and fasting should be done only on appropriate occasions (see Zech. 7:1–7 with 8:18–19), there are similarities in the manner in which both should be observed. The purpose of fasting in Scripture is never for the sake of abstaining from food; that is dieting. The purpose of fasting is to seek the Lord through humiliation and fervent prayer (for example, Neh. 1:4ff).[10]

---

9. Although he does not develop the idea fully and does not address this passage in particular, the seed thought of this connection between fasting and Sabbath-keeping is found in Owen, *Hebrews*, 2: 281.

10. The Puritan Henry Scudder wrote that religious fasting is "sanctifying

This means that a day of fasting would have been ordinarily a day with less labor and activity, so that extra time might be devoted to prayer. Although the purposes of Sabbath-keeping and fasting are so different that they may even be called polar opposites (which is why many have counseled against fasting on the Sabbath),[11] both emphasize the setting aside a day for the purpose of seeking God more directly and exclusively. In this respect, the Sabbath—though a day of worship, feasting, and rejoicing—is the pattern for fast days, as days of worship through humility, mourning, dependence, and even shame (see Dan. 9:1ff). It is important to remember that the Sabbath was the pattern for days of not only fasting, but for everyday religious observance in the Jewish calendar. This is why the Day of Atonement, the feast of trumpets, the feast of tabernacles, and by implication, all Israel's feast and fast days, were called "Sabbaths" (see Lev. 16:31; 23:24, 32, 39) and why the weekly Sabbath was prefaced to the entire list of them (Lev. 23:3). The weekly Sabbath was the permanent *principle* that cast its shadow over and provided the blueprint for every significant event in the Jewish year. Isaiah 58, therefore, moves from the lesser practice of fasting to the greater practice of Sabbath-keeping. We should not assume that all of the terms contained in verses 13–14 must be understood exclusively in terms of verses 1–12. To do so would be like looking at a shadow in order to depict the body that cast it, rather than looking at the body to understand the form of the shadow.

Many read in verses 1–12 about the oppression of laborers and the greed and desire for profit, and they assume it is commerce alone

---

a day to the Lord by a willing abstinence from meat and drink, from delights and worldly labors, that the whole man may be more thoroughly humbled before God, and more fervent in prayer." Henry Scudder, *The Christian's Daily Walk* (repr., Harrisonburg, Va.: Sprinkle Publications, 1984), 49.

11. See for example Richard Baxter, *A Christian Directory* (Grand Rapids: Reformation Heritage Books, 2005). Dabney also cited early church fathers, such as Tertullian, as asserting that because the Sabbath was a day for joy, fasting upon the Sabbath was "wrong." R. L. Dabney, "The Christian Sabbath: Its Nature, Design, and Proper Observance," in *Discussions* (1890; repr., Harrisonburg, Va.: Sprinkle Publications, 1982), 1:537.

God is concerned about in verse 13.[12] They unnecessarily impose the instructions concerning fasting upon the pattern of Sabbath-keeping. Does this not follow from the presupposition that the primary emphasis of the Sabbath is rest from labor rather than worship? If you presuppose that the purpose of the Sabbath is rest, you will see only labor in every prohibition. If, however, you presuppose that God has sanctified one entire day out of seven for Himself, so His creatures may enjoy communion with Him without the distractions of the other six days, you will see much more in this passage than just rest from labor. You will also assume that the commandment forbids any activities that divert or distract you from the duties of public and private worship. Isaiah gives every indication that the original intention of the Sabbath was worship, and that worship should be the controlling factor with respect to our thinking about the Sabbath. If you are not convinced that the accent of the fourth commandment rests upon "Keep it holy," rather than "In it you shall do no labor," then unfortunately it is likely that we shall still speak past one another as we consider the details of verses 13–14. We can understand the meaning and application of Isaiah 58:13–14 only when we approach the text with biblical presuppositions about the purpose of the Sabbath.

---

12. For example, in explaining verse 13, the *Reformation Study Bible* asserts, "Their goals were social prestige, financial gain, and political importance." R. C. Sproul, ed., *The Reformation Study Bible* (Orlando: Ligonier Ministries, 2005), 1035. This may be what *their goals* were, but we cannot assume that the goals of men limit what goals *God* has for Sabbath-keeping. This assertion implies that God cannot do anything other than respond to and correct the errors of men, rather than contrast their ways with positive teaching of His own.

CHAPTER FOUR

Revisiting
Isaiah 58:13–14

When we come to the prohibitions and requirements of Isaiah 58:13–14 with the idea that the purpose of the Sabbath day is the worship of God and communion with His people, then the conclusions of the Westminster Shorter Catechism do not seem so strange. To simplify the discussion of this passage, I will briefly examine the prohibitions under three headings and the requirements under two. The teaching of this passage will provide some practical principles to guide us in our Sabbath-keeping.

Prohibitions and Requirements

The Prohibitions

God commanded the people through Isaiah to *turn away their feet* from the Sabbath. The prominent idea is that they should not trample the Sabbath under their feet (v. 13). The Sabbath is a holy day. As God commanded Moses to take the shoes off his feet, since the place where He manifested His presence was holy ground (Ex. 3:5), so we are commanded not to trample under our feet the day the Lord has "hallowed" for the purposes of worship. In this passage, God gave His people three prohibitions wherein they must not violate the Sabbath: by doing their "own ways," finding their "own pleasure," or by speaking their "own words."

"*Not doing thine own ways.*" The first thing to note about this phrase is that Isaiah did not command the people to abstain from what was inherently sinful on any day. This was obvious and did not need to be said; sin is sin every day, and prohibiting sin has nothing distinctly to do with Sabbath-keeping. Presbyterian William S. Plumer noted:

> Some have suggested that the weekly day of rest under the gospel, which is an eminently spiritual dispensation, is not to be a rest from labor or business, but only from sin. To such it is sufficient to reply, that every day of life ought to be a day of abstinence from all sin: and when it shall be shown that we are at liberty to indulge in sin six days out of seven, and then avoid it for one day only, it will be time enough to make a more serious and extended answer.[1]

For this reason, the "ways" here probably mean the ordinary course of life throughout the week. The Sabbath is God's holy day. It is not a day on which the common activities of life continue uninterrupted: workmen cease from laboring, businessmen forgo business trips, students cease studying, homemakers postpone laundry, and so on. Likewise, when the Shorter Catechism asserts we must lay aside our "worldly" employments and recreations, "worldly" does not mean sinful, but rather ordinary or common.

"*Nor finding thine own pleasure.*" This phrase is mentioned twice in verse 13 for emphasis, and it is a summary of the other prohibitions mentioned in the passage. It means "doing as you please." In the simplest terms, we violate the Sabbath by doing what we please on it, rather than what pleases God. Did you notice that each of the prohibitions in this passage begins with the phrase "thine own"? *Thine own* ways, *thine own* pleasure, and *thine own* words are implicitly contrasted with *God's* ways, *God's* pleasures, and words that please *God*. The Sabbath is *God's* holy day, not *ours*. It is not a day on which we determine what activities please us on our "day off." We must always ask the question, "What pleases God on a day set apart to worship Him?" It is not sufficient to ask, "What is pleasing to God in general?" but rather "What is pleasing to God on this

---

1. William S. Plumer, *The Law of God* (1864; repr., Harrisonburg, Va.: Sprinkle Publications, 1996), 307.

day?" If you view the purpose of the Sabbath as rest from labor, with some duties of worship, you will probably define "thine own pleasures" in terms of your weekly labors and routines. If, however, you view the purpose of the Sabbath as a "holy day" of worship, then you will understand "thine own pleasures" as those not suited to the purposes of the day, no matter how appropriate and lawful they are on the other six days. The requirements contained in Isaiah 58:13 (as we will see) reveal that the reason why we are not to pursue every lawful pleasure on the Lord's Day is because of the greater pleasures God has intended for the day.

The question of recreation on the Sabbath is relevant at this point. This is probably the most commonly rejected aspect of Sabbath-keeping as taught in the Westminster Standards. Why are worldly recreations that are lawful on other days forbidden on the Sabbath? They are forbidden because they are out of accord with the purpose of the day. Many object to this principle on varied grounds. I have heard some say that they are opposed only to "organized sports" on the Sabbath (in favor of "disorganized sports"?), because they may interfere with worship services on the day. Others present a list of seemingly innocent and restful activities they do not consider inappropriate for the Sabbath—such as bicycling, swimming, or playing golf. It seems to me that these objections approach the question of recreation entirely from the wrong perspective. The reason worldly recreations are inconsistent with a day set apart for worship will be made clearer under the treatment of speaking our own words below. For now, the question we ought to be asking about recreation or any other activity on the Sabbath day is not "What is wrong with it?" but rather "How does it promote the purposes of the day?" Anything done for the purpose of rest in itself on the Sabbath is done for the wrong purpose. All that genuinely promotes the worship of God on the Sabbath promotes the purpose of the day.[2] Recreation serves the

---

2. I will go into more detail in chapter 4 in order to illustrate this point. On the question of recreation on the Sabbath, see the insightful article by Lane Keister in *The Confessional Presbyterian Journal* 5 (2009), 229–38.

purpose of diverting our minds *from every other activity.* How can we then view them as anything other than pursuing "what pleases us," rather than what pleases the Lord on His "holy day?"

For most in today's world, the Lord's Day is virtually the only opportunity where we are finally freed from the distractions of entertainment, sports, and business in order to think directly and exclusively about eternal realities. I say "freed" because, although entertainments and recreation can be used moderately to the glory of God, we have come to a place in our culture where they have entirely consumed us. Jonathan Edwards once resolved that he would not say anything "sportive or matter of laughter on the Sabbath day." I initially puzzled over this statement. What Edwards had in mind, however, was that there should be a holy solemnity associated with a day entirely devoted to worshiping the King of kings. The point is not that the day should be without humor and without joy. Some believers, such as Charles Spurgeon, have the ability to use humor in a sanctified manner without detracting from the solemnity of the occasion. The joy of the Sabbath should be of the best kind, since it is the day in which believers exercise the highest privilege God has given. Worldly recreations on the Sabbath are no more appropriate than if a groom paused in the middle of his wedding ceremony to check the scores of a football game. Recreation would be a perfectly appropriate pleasure on a day of rest from labor, but an entirely inappropriate one on a day devoted to taking pleasure in worship.

"Nor speaking thine own words." This is probably the most difficult part of Sabbath-keeping. In every other commandment, we are keenly aware we may violate the law of God in our speech as much as in our actions. But when was the last time you considered how you broke the Sabbath with your words? Is the fourth commandment the only commandment among the ten we cannot violate with our words as well as with our actions? Even if you believe that the purpose of Sabbath-keeping is relegated to rest from labor, do you not still have an obligation to keep the Sabbath in your heart and speech, as well as in your behavior? As a bare minimum, it should be obvious that the Sabbath is not a day for unnecessary speech about

our work. Can you truly say you keep the commandment when your speech is filled with the very activities forbidden by the commandment? This is like a man who keeps himself from the outward act of adultery, but is constantly telling his friends and wife how much he desires other women. Out of the overflow of the heart the mouth speaks (Matt. 15:19–20). If you fill your heart and your speech with worldly employments on the Sabbath, are you truly keeping the Sabbath, even though you might not go to work that day? Is this not the very essence of hypocrisy?

Once again, what about recreation? If your worldly recreation is forbidden on the Sabbath day, is it appropriate to occupy your speech and thoughts with them? What do you communicate when you rush from the place of corporate worship in order to watch the "big game"? On one occasion, I was in the home of a friend for fellowship on the Sabbath, and a visitor was obviously growing impatient over something. When the man could stand it no longer, he went into the living room and turned on the Super Bowl! Most of the rest of us had forgotten it was "Super Bowl Sunday." The result was that a time of heaven-like Christian fellowship was completely negated for the sake of a game no one would be talking about in a month. Yet the things we were talking about we hoped to be occupied with for an eternity! What saddens me is that some of you may be thinking right now, "But it's the Super Bowl!" This illustrates a massive problem with our Christian living that I will address in the next chapter.

It may help you, in part, to look at yourself from the perspective of a nonbeliever. We say that our God is infinite in His glorious perfections, and His perfect justice demands that sinners deserve no less than the eternal torments of hell for being rebels against an eternal Lord. We say further that although it would have been just and right for the Father not to save a single member of the human race from sin and misery, He did so by sending His Son to be fully God and fully man. We profess that Jesus, as the second Adam, stood in our place on the cross and was made sin in the eyes of God, bearing His full wrath and curse, in order that we might become the righteousness of God in Him (2 Cor. 5:21). We affirm that He has saved us by His mercy and not by our works of righteousness, but by receiving His promises through faith (Titus 3:5). Then we tell others that His Spirit dwells in us and that we have the privilege of coming into His presence. We believe that we call him Father only on account of what the Son of God has done for us. We believe that when two or three of us are gathered together in His name, He is there in our midst (Matt. 18:20), and we strive to offer up our lives as living sacrifices in a continual act of spiritual worship (Rom. 12:1–2). Then we pray every week that when we come into corporate worship on the Lord's Day, unbelievers would come into our midst, be convicted of their sin, and fall on their faces saying, "God is truly among you!" (1 Cor. 14:25).

Unfortunately, when the unbeliever comes into our midst, we do not speak about the glories of the Lord and the love of Christ that passes knowledge. Instead, we talk about our golf schedule, who will win the Super Bowl, the coming World Series, or the current score of the soccer game. What should a nonbeliever think when he hears these things? Should we honestly expect him to fall on his face and say that God is among us? Should we expect him to wonder at such a glorious plan of redemption, and how this glorious God has changed these people? Should we expect him to believe that we have just entered into the Holy of Holies in heaven, when our minds are so obviously resting in the sanctuary of our recreation? Does this not make it obvious why recreation is incompatible with a day of worship? And what does it say about us if we freely converse on the Lord's Day as if we are little affected by the presence of God, but quickly seek to alter our behavior and speech when an unknown visitor shows up? And what about the suffering widow who survives each week by looking forward to the edifying fellowship she will enjoy with her brethren on the first day of that week? What about the man of God who is so wearied by the strains of his demanding job that he crawls into the pew on the Lord's Day, longing for solace and hungering for glory? I promise you that, regardless of their convictions regarding the Sabbath (or your own), you are grieving these people and doing them disservice by your lack of spiritual conversation on the Sabbath. There are few things that demonstrate more vividly how little we believe our Christianity than the conversations heard among God's people before and after corporate worship. This applies not only to corporate worship, but also to the entire day, which is sanctified to the Lord. It is necessary for you to recognize how you may completely destroy the blessings of the Sabbath (and corporate worship) for yourselves as well as for others by thoughtless speech and conversation.

The Requirements

The requirements of Sabbath-keeping in Isaiah 58:13 are summarized by the phrase, "Call the Sabbath a delight." Notice the glory of this command! You are not told, "This commandment is difficult, but you must endure it." You are not commanded to set aside your own pleasures for the sake of a day of boring drudgery. You are required to call the day honorable by delighting in the day! In other words, you cannot keep the Sabbath properly unless it is a joy for you to do so.

The joy of the Sabbath day is intimately tied to the purpose of the day. There is a problem when men attempt to recommend Sabbath-keeping to others on the grounds of the physical and mental benefits that come from keeping a day of rest. B. B. Warfield correctly implied that appeals of this kind are the best way to lose the Sabbath entirely.[3] On this basis, any delight in the day will be distinctively man-centered rather than God-centered. Walter Chantry noted, "Perhaps there are great psychological and physical benefits to be received from not spending all our days in similar activity. Nevertheless, *the intent of the day is not rest*, absolutely considered. It is rest from our works so that we may give ourselves to the Lord

---

3. This is implied by the reasons for which he wrote his article. While other men were defending the Sabbath on the basis of its benefits, Warfield defended it by rooting it in Scripture. B. B. Warfield, "The Foundations of the Sabbath in the Word of God," in *Selected Shorter Writings,* ed. John E. Meeter (Phillipsburg, N.J.: P&R, 1970), 1:308–9.

on that day."[4] The positive requirement of Sabbath-keeping in Isaiah 58:13 may be summarized as, "Delight in God through worship, and do so for one whole day out of seven."

Too often we are not proactive enough in keeping the commandments of God. As long as we do the bare minimum of not working, is it not true that we derisively accuse those who press any further obligations as giving us a list of "do's" and "don'ts"? Ironically, however, if you take such a position, your Sabbath-keeping will be passive and negative in nature. Christian living should always have a distinctively positive focus. If we sought to occupy the entire day with the public and private exercises of God's worship, then the rest of our questions with regard to what is and what is not lawful on the Sabbath would solve themselves. If we truly believe we have come from the heavenly sanctuary and from worshiping the true and living God in an innumerable company of angels, will we desire to speak about our jobs? Would we have the slightest care about sporting events? Are we so little affected by coming into the presence of the Father, through the Son, by the power of the Holy Spirit that we would rather rush to our recreation than observe a day of worship? Do we have such a low view of God that He is not worthy of our undivided attention for twenty-four hours? The Sabbath was made for man, but man was made for God. The Sabbath was made for man in order that he might have one whole day in seven to pursue what is most profitable to his soul, and it is the source of the greatest of all pleasures in this life and the next: worship and communion with God.

Some Significant Objections

The weightiest of objections I have encountered against the above interpretation of Isaiah 58 are well presented by R. C. Sproul. Sproul demonstrates a thorough understanding of the teaching of

---

4. Walter Chantry, *Call the Sabbath a Delight* (Edinburgh: Banner of Truth, 1991), 22 (emphasis original).

the Westminster Standards on the Sabbath, and he has treated the subject with sympathy and honesty. He argues that the Puritans' position on the Sabbath is based upon a faulty view of the term "pleasure," in which they inferred that recreation and other lawful pleasures were forbidden on the Sabbath day. He argues that it was commercial profits that were in view rather than "pleasures" such as recreation. The crux of his objection, however, is the assertion that if this interpretation of this passage is correct, then Isaiah would have added to the requirements of the Mosaic Law. Yet this was not the role of Israel's prophets. They were not legislators, but prosecuting attorneys. In other words, their role was not as lawgivers, but as reformers. Sproul asserts that prior to Isaiah, there is no place in the law in which recreation is forbidden on the Sabbath; therefore, it would be inconsistent with the role of the prophets for Isaiah to intend this in this passage.[5]

The strength of Sproul's position is twofold. First, he does not (as so many others) plead a laxity or abrogation of the law under the New Testament, but argues that the law *never* forbade recreation on the Sabbath. Second, he deals with the Puritan position fairly, kindly, and, at points, even sympathetically. In my opinion, Sproul's grounds for objecting that the Sabbath excludes recreation are the only ones that do justice to and are consistent with the Reformed view of the continuity of the law of God. As the weight of this objection is placed upon the Westminster position regarding recreation, the position is not crushed by its weight for two important reasons.

First, it is not true that the law never forbade thoughts, words, and works concerning our worldly employments and recreations on the Sabbath. It is true that there is no *explicit* command to this effect in the law, yet the law did require it by "good and necessary consequence" (see Westminster Confession 1.6). *Inferences* drawn legitimately from Scripture have the same binding force as explicit commands. The applications of some commandments are explicitly

5. R. C. Sproul, *Truths We Confess: A Layman's Guide to the Westminster Confession of Faith* (Phillipsburg, N.J.: P&R, 2007), 2:343–44.

spelled out at a later time, which were necessarily implied when they were first given. For example, God always intended marriage to be monogamous rather than polygamous. It is also true that He has always hated divorce. Yet the latter was not explicitly stated in the law, but by the prophet Malachi, and the former was not made overt until the coming of Christ! The creation ordinance of marriage necessarily implied both of these truths, and God's people were expected to abide by them, even though they failed miserably in both. In the same manner, rather than adding to the law of God, Isaiah spelled out explicitly the "necessary consequence" implicit in the creation ordinance of the Sabbath. Therefore, while the criteria that Sproul demands in interpreting this passage are legitimate and helpful, his conclusions are not sound. By implication, "taking up the entire time in the public and private exercises of God's worship" excludes worldly employments and recreation that are lawful on other days.

Second, Sproul's assertion concerning the meaning of the term "pleasures" confuses the application of a principle with the principle itself. Prohibiting labor on the Sabbath is one *application* of the command not to do our "own pleasures" on the Sabbath. Work is a gift of God that should be a "pleasure" to us as we do it to the Lord and not to men (Col. 3:23–24). Christians should love to work, yet even a job that is a "pleasure" is to be set aside on the day that is designed for worship and communion with God and His people exclusively. The people in Isaiah's time may not have taken "pleasure" in their labor for godly reasons, but merely for the profit they sought from their labors; yet even if "pleasures" in this context refers directly to commerce only, the term still bears the meaning of "doing as you please." In this case, what pleased them was the profit they gained from commerce. However, the *principle* that God cited against them was that they should not do whatever pleased them on the Sabbath, but rather what was pleasing to Him, the terms of which are spelled out in the passage. Not doing anything we please is the *principle* of Sabbath-keeping enforced by Isaiah. Forbidding the pursuit of profit by means of commerce on the Sabbath is one *example* of how this principle should be applied. In effect, Sproul has implied that the principle of Sabbath-keeping is exhausted in a single application. This amounts to saying, "As long as I do not engage in commerce, I have not done my own pleasures on the Sabbath." However, is this not the same error as those who say, "As long as I have not killed anyone, I am not guilty of violating the sixth commandment?" It is characteristic of the Bible to give general principles with a few specific examples of application that are designed to guide us to make further applications of these principles. This is what the Westminster divines did when they asserted that "pleasures" excluded lawful recreation from the Sabbath as well as lawful labor. The true pleasures of the Sabbath are not rest and recreation, but worship and communion with God.

The Significance of the Promises

The last important consideration is the promises attached to the Sabbath. A mentor and friend of mine likes to present the blessings promised in Isaiah 58:14 in such a manner that we should be willing to do whatever it takes to have them. We should covet and long for the blessings of verse 14, and we should view no task too great in order to enjoy them. The promises attached to Sabbath-keeping are summarized in three particulars, of which I can skim only the surface here.

"Then shalt thou delight thyself in the Lord." This blessing is understood immediately and appeals intuitively to the heart of a weary and sin-laden believer. Have you not been grieved many times at how little you delight in the Lord? Do you not mourn that you have so little love for Him who first loved you and gave Himself for you? Delighting in the Lord is simultaneously one of the greatest and most elusive blessings of the Christian life. What believer would deny that his greatest joys have been those times when he has tasted and seen that the Lord is good? How blessed and necessary it is to find great delight in Him who is the fountain of life, in whose presence is fullness of joy, and at whose right hand are pleasures

forevermore! God has promised delight in Him as a benefit of Sabbath-keeping. This results from the preparation that attends anticipating a day of worship, from intensely meditating on the resurrection of the Savior, from the benefits of corporate worship and fellowship, and from God's blessing upon each of these beyond their own intrinsic value on the Sabbath.

"And I will cause thee to ride upon the high places of the earth." In Deuteronomy 32:12–13 and 33:29, this language describes the victory of God's people over their enemies.[6] The Scriptures apply this not only to physical victory over enemies. Habakkuk asserted that God would make him walk on His high hills (Hab. 3:19), even *in the midst* of the worst kind of adversity. For this prophet, the "high hills" are a symbolic depiction of the triumph the prophet enjoyed through faith in the promises and goodness of God. This is likely the meaning in Isaiah 58:14. By delighting in the Sabbath, God promises to cause your faith to flourish and your soul to prosper by His blessing. When the church as a whole delights in the Sabbath, this promise will undoubtedly do much to promote and further the spiritual mission of the church in seeking the salvation of the nations.

"And feed thee with the heritage of Jacob thy father." To be fed with an inheritance is to enjoy the benefits of that inheritance. Though few of us are physical descendents of Abraham, Isaac, and Jacob, by faith we are the children of Abraham (Gal. 3:7, 29). God has promised that those who honor the Sabbath will enjoy the full benefits of the covenant of grace. Pipa writes, "Our inheritance includes the benefits of salvation: adoption, assurance of salvation, boldness in prayer, confidence. This promise means we will revel in our privileges as children of God. These benefits are not merely a list of privileges to memorize; they are spiritual pleasures to be enjoyed—the everyday practical participation in your privileges as a child of God."[7]

---

6. Pipa, *Lord's Day*, 12; Harman, *Isaiah*, 388.
7. Pipa, *Lord's Day*, 13–14.

There are *intrinsic* advantages to sanctifying a day for worship and communion with God and His people, without the distractions of worldly employments and recreation. These promises in Isaiah 58:14 are astonishing in that God has added special promises to activities that inherently bless His people. The duties of the Sabbath are duties that ought to delight the hearts of believers every day of the week. How much more when God has added promises to them on one day out of seven? If we *cannot* delight in the duties of worship for a whole day, then we may have deeper spiritual problems than Sabbath-breaking. Chantry asked, "How can the day be a day of pleasure unless we rejoice in the Lord? But then how can we rejoice in the Lord if a day of worshiping him is a heaviness to us? The condition and the hope are bound together and mutually supportive."[8]

What disturbs me more than the fact that so many have forgotten the biblical basis for the teaching of the Westminster Standards on the Sabbath is the hostile, and almost violent, reaction of many to the very *suggestion* that they should take one entire day of rest from labor and recreation in order to worship and commune with God. Should not your bias be in favor of a day of worship rather than against it? Should you not *desire* that God give you such a day, and be disappointed if you found out that there was no such thing? Years ago, I had a good friend who was a dispensationalist. He did not believe that the fourth commandment was binding upon Christians in any sense. However, after explaining to him the purpose of the Lord's Day, the intrinsic value of the day for believers, and the glorious promises of Isaiah 58:14, he confessed that he actually envied my conviction! He *longed* for the conviction that God had required such a day with such glorious promises. In fact, he began to meet with me and a few others every Lord's Day so he could enjoy the inherent blessings of Sabbath-keeping, even though he could not lay hold of the promises attached to a day he did not believe existed. He actually desired a day of worship *more* than his worldly employments, and even his recreation! My friend did not covet only

---

8. Chantry, *Call the Sabbath a Delight*, 38.

the *promises* attached to the day; he coveted the Puritan *concept* of the day. Oh that God would give His people a bias in favor of the Sabbath. When He does so in the church at large, we will probably conclude that revival has come at last.

Conclusions

The reason believers often speak past one another when discussing Sabbath-keeping relates to how they understand the purpose of the day. The question of whether we presuppose that the Sabbath is intended for rest or that the solemn worship of God is *the determinative factor* guides our interpretation of Isaiah 58:13–14. I have sought to remedy this problem by dragging our presuppositions out into the open, and by seeing which ones fit the overall teaching of Scripture, and Isaiah in particular. I admit that my exposition of Isaiah 58 is guided by my presuppositions about the Sabbath day, since it cannot be otherwise.

In light of what has been said above, the first important observation is that you cannot call the Sabbath a delight unless you are a Christian. By a Christian, I mean a person who is in union with Christ. By union with Christ, the Scriptures mean that all that Christ is and has done, He is and has done for you. The way you receive the benefits of Christ's death and resurrection is through faith in His promises. God has promised that as many as receive Him to them He gives the power to become the children of God (John 1:12). If you have not come to God by grace alone, through faith alone, in Christ alone, then you have no fellowship with God. No one comes to the Father except through the Son (John 14:6). As a creature of God, you are obligated to refrain from work on the Sabbath, but until God makes you a new creature in Christ, you cannot enjoy fellowship with Him and His people on the Sabbath. May God grant that each of you know the Lord of the Sabbath, and that in knowing Him you may have life in His name.

Second, this passage contains an important message for the church. Many of us have a great hope that God would once again pour out times of refreshing from His presence, that He would revive us again so we can rejoice and be glad in Him, that He would increase the personal godliness and zeal of His people and bring many nonbelievers into His kingdom by the Holy Spirit blessing the Word of God and the witness of His people for their eternal salvation. In short, we recognize the need for and long for genuine revival. Some have even begun to call for "solemn assemblies" of fasting and prayer, and they have urged the church to give the Lord no rest until He has mercy upon us.[9] Why are we fasting and praying? Is it not that others and we should delight ourselves in the Lord, that the church would ride on the heights of the earth and be victorious in her mission, and that God would feed His people with the heritage of Jacob their father? I do not mean in the least to discourage fasting and prayer for revival, but is this not the Israelites' very problem in Isaiah 58? They were fasting and praying, but God questioned them about their *Sabbath-keeping*. Do we seek the Lord to revive His church? Let us fast and pray together, but let us first and foremost call the Sabbath a delight. Let us lay hold of the promises attached to Sabbath-keeping, that God might visit us with the showers of His blessings. There is more at stake in Sabbath-breaking than the curse of God; Sabbath-breaking deprives God's people of some of the most blessed and glorious promises in Scripture! Recovering the Sabbath day may even coincide with a revival of biblical Christianity. May God grant us mercy to repent of our Sabbath-breaking and to pray earnestly for the blessings attached to the day. In doing so, the Lord may revive His church. Then we shall delight ourselves in the Lord. Then we shall ride on the heights of the earth. Then God shall feed us with the heritage of Jacob our father. "The mouth of the Lord hath spoken it."

---

9. For example, Richard Owen Roberts has produced a useful compilation of sermons and addresses from numerous American Puritans on this very issue. He has included a useful essay of his own on the use of solemn assemblies and their connection with revivals, both biblically and historically. Richard Owen Roberts, ed., *Sanctify the Congregation: A Call to the Solemn Assembly and Corporate Repentance* (Wheaton, Ill.: International Awakening Press, 1994).

CHAPTER FIVE

Worldliness

As men get older, they often believe they are in better physical condition than they are. They become unwilling to acknowledge signs of strain and fatigue when they are engaged in physical labor. They want to believe that nothing has changed and that they are able to do and accomplish as much as they did when they were young men. This results from not only increased age, but also lack of exercise. For example, a man who ran in marathons when he was younger can no longer do so if he has not kept his body in good physical condition. Nothing shows the man the extent of the change in his physical condition more than if he attempts to run a marathon without training for it. Just as running in a marathon serves as a good indicator of a man's physical condition, so the Sabbath is a good indicator of his spiritual condition. If a man is in poor spiritual health, then attempting to sanctify an entire day to the Lord for public and private worship will end in the same results as an out-of-shape runner in a marathon; in both cases, the results will be painful.

Striving to keep the Sabbath day holy may reveal that we are out of shape spiritually. Worldliness, or earthly mindedness, may be the underlying cause. The difficulty of laying aside all unnecessary thoughts, words, and works about our worldly employments and recreations for an entire day often uncovers the fact that the church has loved the world and the things in the world in an inordinate manner. Although this book is primarily about the Sabbath, no doctrine or practice in Scripture can be considered in isolation. I am convinced that the modern aversion to keeping the Sabbath holy is, in part, a result of improper love for the world and a mistaken view of Christian living. The duties of the Sabbath serve as an irritant, aggravating the worldliness that has crept into the hearts and lives of God's people.

This chapter examines the nature and causes of worldliness, which often result from the abuse of basic principles of Christian living. The next chapter concludes the topic of worldliness with some characteristics of healthy Christian living, coupled with the fact that the church today is often put to shame by the piety that God required of Israel. The Christian's struggle with the biblical concept of the Sabbath and the out-of-shape runner collapsing in the middle of a marathon both reveal that the problem is not with the race, but with the runner.

The Nature and Causes of Worldliness

A man or a woman pursuing a career in medicine spends a good deal of time studying the nature and symptoms of various diseases before he or she begins diagnosing patients. Similarly, in order to connect the symptom of the widespread neglect of the day of worship to the disease of worldliness, it is important to begin by studying the nature of the disease. Joel Beeke has described worldliness in this manner: "Worldliness...is human activity without God."[1] In other words, a worldly life is a life lived without reference to God. The worldly man is like the fool in Psalm 14:1 who says in his heart, "There is no God." This does not mean, however, that everyone who is worldly is a professed atheist. Worldliness may take the form of what has been called "practical atheism," in which a man *lives* as if there were no God, regardless of what he believes.[2] The human heart is deceitful and desperately wicked (Jer. 17:9). Worldliness may take

---

1. Joel R. Beeke, *A Loving Encouragement to Flee Worldliness* (Grand Rapids: Reformation Heritage Books, 2002), 2.

2. For an extended treatment of "practical atheism," see the classic work by Stephen Charnock, *The Existence and Attributes of God* (n.d.; repr., Grand Rapids: Baker, 2000), 89–175.

shape in a life lived in the name of God, while the *mind* and *affections* are upon the things of this world. Whatever form worldliness takes, in essence it involves inordinate love for the things of this world. Worldliness may be present in believers to a greater or lesser degree. Therefore, they must be warned against it, and search themselves for it. Then again, worldliness utterly consumes nonbelievers; it is the *characteristic* trait of their lives. The warning of the apostle John against worldliness appeals to both of these groups: "Love not the world, neither the things that are in the world. If any man love the world, the love of the Father is not in him. For all that is in the world, the lust of the flesh, and the lust of the eyes, and the pride of life, is not of the Father, but is of the world" (1 John 2:15–16).[3]

A worldly man or woman may possess great zeal for religion. Although worldliness is the opposite of heavenly mindedness, ironically, a worldly man or woman may be intensely religious and have hopes of entering heaven. The Pharisees are the prime example of this type of worldliness. The apostle Paul asserted that the Jews had "a zeal for God" (Rom. 10:2), though not according to knowledge. The Pharisees were the strictest sect of the Jewish religion (Acts 26:5). Living as a Pharisee, Paul exceeded his peers in zeal (Phil. 3:4–6). Later in life, however, he referred to his former religious life as ignorant and unbelieving (1 Tim. 1:13). The Pharisees were characterized by misguided zeal, coupled with loving the world and the things in the world. Have you noticed that most of the teaching concerning *covetousness* in the Gospel of Luke is directed against the Pharisees? There is no sin that exhibits the spirit of the world and no sin so deeply rooted in the human heart as covetousness. In Luke 12, Jesus said, "Beware of the leaven of the Pharisees, which is hypocrisy" (v. 1). The remainder of the chapter implicitly illustrates the hypocrisy of the Pharisees almost exclusively in terms of covetousness and anxiety over earthly possessions. This section is

3. The term "world" has many significations in Scripture. In a sense, I am including all of them under the discussion of worldliness. Whether we consider the world as sinful human beings and their way of life or simply the physical things in this world, worldliness is always an inordinate love for the world.

preceded by a series of "woes" pronounced against the Pharisees and the experts in the law (11:37–54). After warning the disciples to avoid such hypocrisy, Jesus taught them to fear God rather than men (12:4–12). In the parables and teaching that follow, Luke has arranged his material with great theological skill in order to illustrate the worldly behavior that characterized the scribes, Pharisees, and experts in the Jewish law.

First, a man came pleading with Jesus to arbitrate a dispute between him and his brother over dividing their inheritance (v. 13). Surprisingly, Jesus replied, "Take heed, and beware of covetousness" (v. 15). He then illustrated the danger facing those who trust in wealth with the parable of the "rich fool," who filled his barns without tending to his soul. Jesus concluded this parable by observing: "So is he that layeth up treasure for himself, and is not rich toward God" (v. 21). In verses 22 through 34, Jesus transitioned naturally from a discussion about covetousness to anxiety over the outward provisions of life. According to Jeremiah Burroughs, there are two reasons for anxiety over the things of this life: fear that some great evil shall fall upon us and deprive us of something we value, and the fear that we shall not have the means to prevent such evils.[4] Behind this lies the fact that our happiness rests in the things that we possess rather than in the Maker of heaven and earth, and that we have taken the care of our possessions into our own hands. This implicitly relinquishes God's right to protect us and to provide for the things we need. For these reasons, Jesus encouraged the disciples by reminding them of both God's power over all things and of His personal concern for them. If they rested upon these truths, they would be freed to seek first the kingdom of God and His righteousness, trusting that all other things would be added to them (v. 31). These instructions are in direct contrast to the parable of the "rich fool," whose hope, trust, and happiness were his riches. These incidents exposed the hypocrisy of the Pharisees. The remainder of the

---

4. Jeremiah Burroughs, *A Treatise of Earthly Mindedness* (1649; repr., Orlando: Soli Deo Gloria, 2006), 11–12.

chapter teaches Christ's disciples how to seek first the kingdom and its righteousness, while looking to the coming of the Lord.

The Pharisees were a deeply religious people, yet they were hypocrites due to an inordinate love of the world through covetous hearts. They were like the "rich fool" who was rich towards himself but not toward God. On a later occasion, following another parable, Jesus told His disciples that they could not love God and money (Luke 16:13). Luke then commented: "And the Pharisees also, who were covetous, heard all these things: and they derided him" (v. 14). The same love for the world, which led to their covetousness and anxiety, led them to love the praise of men more than the praise of God (John 12:43). This was why they did their good deeds to be seen by men. This same principle caused them to love prominent positions (Luke 14:17–24), and to be resentful when God blessed those whom they thought were undeserving (15:25–32). The Pharisees were highly esteemed by the common people, and they had a good reputation as religious leaders and instructors of the ignorant. However, they illustrate the principle of worldliness with impeccable precision. It is not so much the *activities* we are engaged in that make us worldly, as the spirit in which we engage in them that makes us worldly. It is no wonder Jesus concluded, "Ye are they which justify yourselves before men; but God knoweth your hearts: for what is highly esteemed among men is abomination in the sight of God" (Luke 16:15).

It is easy to regard the Pharisees as "the bad guys" in the Gospels and to assume that their example is so repulsive and so notorious that we have little danger of being like them. This highlights the danger of caricaturing people. It robs us of the benefits of learning from their example, since we conceive of them in a manner that cannot touch us. People are often ready to accuse others of Pharisaism, but they seldom suspect that they may be guilty of it themselves. Jesus went to great lengths to demonstrate the hypocrisy and earthly minded religion of the Pharisees, precisely due to the fact that so few people suspected them of this crime. The point that connects us to the Pharisees is that though they were intensely religious, they had an inordinate affection for the things of this world, and that no one suspected this (including them) until our Lord exposed them. In light of these things, worldliness or earthly mindedness can manifest itself in a thousand different forms: continual anxiety over the future, hoarding wealth, love of popularity, an inordinate preoccupation with sports, being consumed by hobbies, living for entertainment, indulging too much during leisure time, doing things because they are "lawful" rather than for the glory of God, and so forth. The primary *symptoms* of worldliness are a sluggishness and lack of joy and stamina in genuine acts of spiritual worship.[5]

These examples reveal an insidious fact: a man or woman does not necessarily have to be involved in notorious acts of sin immediately obvious to all (such as murder, adultery, robbery, blasphemy, and so on) in order to be "worldly." Paul noted in Philippians that there were many in the church who were "enemies of the cross of Christ" (Phil. 4:18). The end of these people was destruction, their God was their belly, and they gloried in what ought to have put them to shame (v. 19). What characterized the lives of people who lived in this dreadful condition? Paul tells us: "Who set their mind on earthly things." This state of mind is in conflict with the hope of true believers, whose citizenship is in heaven, and who are eagerly awaiting the coming of the Savior for resurrection and judgment (vv. 20–21).

The Sabbath Exposes Worldliness

The problem with worldliness is that it lies in the heart and, like terminal cancer, it is discovered only by tracing outward symptoms to the root cause. Worldliness may be uncovered through many symptoms;

---

5. In an insightful book on prayer, Austin Phelps wrote, "Mental ease is a refined and seductive idol, which often beguiles men who have too much Christian principle, or too much delicacy of nature, or too much prudence of self-control, or it may be too much pride of character, to fall into a physical vice." Austin Phelps, *The Still Hour: Communion with God in Prayer* (1859; repr., Vestavia Hills, Ala.: Solid Ground Christian Books, 2005), 83.

lack of delight in the Sabbath as a day of worship is one of them. The response of the church to Sabbath-keeping often reveals that we have become too consumed with the affairs of this world. We have become too absorbed with our weekly activities and recreations. When we must set them aside for one whole day in seven, we are offended and do not see how we can delight in such a day. Actually, we begin to feel implicitly how spiritually out of shape we are, and like an untrained runner, we want to stop running before our hearts burst.

Worldly or earthly minded men may be well exercised in the things of this world, but attempting to keep the Sabbath holy to the Lord demonstrates their tremendous *spiritual* weakness. Jeremiah Burroughs gave this challenge:

> I wish you would try once to spend one Sabbath exactly and see what a weariness that would be to you. Resolve just one Sabbath to rise early in the morning, and to have your thoughts spiritual and heavenly as much as you can. Then get up and pray alone in your closet. Then read, hear, and meditate, and mark what you hear. And when you go home, think of it and confer about it. And when you come again to attend on the Word, and so spend the whole day in hearing, reading, meditating, and conferencing about good things, calling your family to account, and praying again, see how tiresome this will be to your hearts if they are carnal.[6]

One point that argues in favor of the Westminster position on Sabbath-keeping is that only believers can strive to keep it. A day devoted to worshiping the God of Scripture through His Son Jesus Christ can be attractive only to a regenerated soul under the operative power of the Holy Spirit. The "Puritan" Sabbath can be a joy to a person who is in union and communion with the triune God. It is easy for people to attend a church service faithfully every week, but who could possibly delight in striving to think and speak of little else for an entire day than the glories of God and of His redemption, other than one who has taken God as his greatest portion and

---

6. Burroughs, *Earthly Mindedness*, 18.

delight in heaven and earth (Ps. 73:25–26)? You must be born of the Spirit of God and live by faith in the Son of God even to consider such a task. In other words, loving the Sabbath as a day of worship is not possible for an unconverted person.

This does not mean, however, that everyone struggling with the Sabbath is not a believer in Christ. It also does not mean that everyone who takes a position regarding Sabbath-keeping other than the one presented in this book is ungodly or a worldly Pharisee. As Owen noted, although a different position regarding Sabbath-keeping may be to the great loss of those who hold to it, we do not mean to cast doubt upon the personal godliness of anyone for holding a different position.[7] They may lose the tremendous blessings that are attached to the Sabbath day, yet in every other respect be exemplary Christians and beloved brethren in the Lord.

Although I am writing this book in defense of the Westminster position on Sabbath-keeping, in a sense it does not matter what view you take at this juncture. For a true Christian, should it not be *natural* to devote at least one whole day in seven exclusively to the worship and service of God? If you attempt to do so, it will tell you a lot about yourself. It will reveal to you, at least in some measure, how much you love the world and the things in the world and how much you must grow in love to your God and Savior. Regardless of your position on the Sabbath, if you try to keep it as a day of worship, it may show that you have a deeper problem and that your affection for this world holds more sway in your heart than you previously thought. No man can serve two masters. He shall inevitably love the one and hate the other. In like manner, no man who loves the world and the things in the world can love the Sabbath or the Lord of the Sabbath; if he loves the world, he shall hate the Sabbath. Many may never know there is a problem until they strive to keep an entire day holy to the Lord.

---

7. John Owen, "The Grace and Duty of Being Spiritually Minded," in *The Works of John Owen* (London, 1681; repr., Edinburgh: Banner of Truth, 1994), 7:331.

An Abuse of Principles

Although Sabbath-keeping exposes worldliness, there is an enormous obstruction in the vision of many that hinders their ability to see this fact. Strangely, worldliness has crept into the church through an abuse of otherwise biblical principles. Perhaps this is not so strange, however. After all, when Satan sought to tempt Jesus in the wilderness, he did so by means of misapplying the principles contained in several passages of Scripture (Matt. 4:1–11).[8] Jesus was not so easily fooled; He was the Son of God, and He endured temptation perfectly so that He might be qualified to be the Savior of the world. Yet the church is always subject to the danger of being deceived as long as her members are on this side of glory. One point at which the modern church has been led astray is that it is increasingly popular to erase distinctions between worship and everything else that we do.

Many believers are beginning either to intentionally or implicitly assume that Romans 12:1–2 reduces every activity in life to the same common denominator. In this text, we are told that in light of the mercies of God in Christ, we must present our bodies as living sacrifices, which are holy and acceptable to God. According to Paul, this is your spiritual worship. There is good reason to regard this text as a "key" to Christian living, since it is all-encompassing and touches everything we set our hands to. Christians must worship God through Jesus Christ in every activity of life. They must worship God at the office, when working in the garden, in their sports, in their recreations, and even when resting in their sleep. If worldliness is "a life without respect to God," these verses demand a life that regards God in everything. For this reason, Burroughs boldly asserted that a spiritually minded man is more "spiritual" in digging ditches than an earthly minded or worldly man is in prayer,

---

8. "Through the 'deceitfulness of sin' divine truth is often changed into a lie; and this in exact proportion to its importance in the salvation of the soul. Satan is never so dangerous a foe as when he poses as an angel of light, and becomes the seeming advocate of truth." B. M. Palmer, *The Threefold Fellowship and the Threefold Assurance: An Essay in Two Parts* (n.d.; repr., Harrisonburg, Va.: Sprinkle Publications, 1980), 143.

hearing sermons, or observing the Lord's Supper.[9] In an ironic twist, Romans 12:1–2, which perhaps above all others militates *against* worldliness, has been distorted to justify a type of Christianity that is heavily imbalanced in its use of this present world.

Many people understand this principle in a manner that undermines the very principle itself. They assert that because all of life should be lived as spiritual worship to God, we must categorically cease to speak of "worship" in a more narrow sense. The result is that what is acceptable every day of the week is also acceptable in the context of what we call "worship" on Sundays. The idea is that what we do during the week may be done on the Lord's Day as well, as long as we are careful to do it as "worship" to the Lord. Some people have adopted this position in practice without self-consciously recognizing a theological shift. However, many modern books on worship are providing a theological framework to support and sustain this shift. I have not cited these works here; the omission is intentional. I do not intend to vilify any particular author or group of authors. Some of these authors have many useful writings, and I do not intend to create a bias against them. My contention is that a major theological shift in the very concept of worship has promoted, and even justified, worldliness among professing Christians. Losing the Sabbath as a day of worship is an inevitable result.

The blurring of corporate worship with everything else has inadvertently diminished the importance of the Sabbath as a day of worship. If you cannot distinguish corporate worship from the rest of life, then surely you cannot distinguish a day set apart for worship from the rest of life. In a sense, this theory treats every day as a Sabbath of worship to the Lord. If any distinction is made between the Lord's Day and every other day, it is only to allow a little more rest on that day from the toil of the week. If carried out consistently, these assertions would negate the importance of private prayer, Bible reading, and family worship as well. If the principle that all of life must be lived to the glory of God demands the erasure of distinctions

9. Burroughs, *Earthly Mindedness*, 16.

between the various activities of life, then it is a small step (if not a necessary one) to conclude that as long as we engage in activities that fall generally within the realm of what is acceptable to God, it does not matter in what activities we occupy our time. If the distinction between worship and the rest of life is lost, a living and vibrant Christian church must go with it. An analogy may help: I may do many projects around our home because I love my wife, yet if I love her only through household projects and never set aside those projects in order to spend time with her and to enjoy her fellowship, we will have a poor excuse for a marriage. Likewise, anyone claiming to worship God in all of life who does not set aside time for direct acts of worship and communion with God will have a poor excuse for a Christian life. Dedicating one whole day in seven to the one relationship that is our reason for existence should be a bare minimum for a Christian. Those who either explicitly or implicitly erase the distinction between direct acts of corporate worship and everything else do not realize that they are in danger of abolishing the foundations of a thriving Christianity. R. L. Dabney illustrated this point well:

> A creature subject to the law of habit, finite in his faculties, compelled by the conditions of his existence to divide his cares between earth and heaven, cannot accomplish his destiny without an authoritative distribution of his time between two worlds. When we remember that men are now carnal and by nature ungodly, ever prone to avert their eyes from heaven to earth; when we see so much of mundane affection, so much of the eager craving and bustle of worldliness, enticing to an infringement on the claims of heaven, we see the absolute necessity of such a division.[10]

This assertion does not set up a false dichotomy by arguing that direct acts of religious worship are the only manner in which we serve God truly. It is a simple observation as much as it is an assertion. Dabney has merely presented the practical reality of the manner in which believers relate to this world. Those who deny the

---

10. Dabney, "Christian Sabbath," 1:542.

distinction between corporate worship and everything else and who deny there is any necessity of setting aside one day out of seven exclusively for worship have lost some practical appreciation of the depravity that remains in the hearts of believers and their tendency to love the world and the things in the world. Perhaps an unfallen man or woman *could* engage in every activity of life in a spirit of worship to the glory of God, but what hope does this provide for sinners? However, even Adam and Eve needed a Sabbath in Paradise. If people professing faith in Christ ignore these facts, is it any wonder that so many who bear the name of Christ seem to live as though they were made for this world only? The fact that the church of Jesus Christ has neglected a day she was meant to set apart for worship is a great sin against great love. The fact, however, that so many of God's people do not see the need for a day of worship, and even have an aversion to one, uncovers a problem, the magnitude of which defies description or exaggeration.

I have known several families that have taken this "all of life is worship" position and, subsequently, a low view of the Sabbath as the day for worship. In one instance, a parent took a job that was a "work of necessity" on the Sabbath day. This was not a problem in and of itself, but soon this person was not disturbed in the least when she began to work every Sabbath day. She justified this by pointing to the fact that she was technically not breaking the Sabbath and that she could worship God just as well at work as she could with the congregation. Eventually, she began to languish spiritually without realizing it. Her Christian faith and walk slowly diminished in every respect, and she became a less effective witness for Christ in her home as well as at work. If you attempt to live in such a way that you do not have at least one day per week to tone your spiritual muscles intensely, instead of always trying to put those muscles to work and perform "secular" tasks in a spiritual manner, then your spiritual vitality will be diminished. It is the mercy of the Lord alone if you do not atrophy entirely. Daily private worship, though indispensable, will not fill the void left by the absence of Sabbath-keeping, neither will family worship. For that matter, attending church for an hour or two a week on Sundays will not be sufficient to sustain your spiritual health. You need intense spiritual exercise to be heavenly minded. Nothing other than a day of rest from worldly employments and recreations, even in your thoughts and speech, to be taken up with the public and private exercises of God's worship can provide you with the spiritual strength and growth you need.

If we do not regard the Sabbath as basic and pivotal to Christian living, we run the risk of doing whatever pleases us throughout the week, while reassuring our consciences that we are not guilty of worldliness because we attach the label of "worship" to everything. In order to present our bodies to God as living sacrifices in spiritual worship, we must habitually and increasingly have a sense of what constitutes pure, undistracted, and unadulterated worship and communion with God. This alone leads us to worship God in every other area of life with our minds set upon things above, where Christ is seated at the right hand of God, rather than upon those things that perish with the using. Sabbath-keeping demonstrates whether or not we have perverted Romans 12:1–2 into a justification for a worldly Christianity. A man cannot live a life of spiritual worship to God if he cannot first enjoy the spiritual worship of God. "To be carnally minded is death, but to be spiritually minded is life and peace" (Rom. 8:6). By diminishing the distinction between direct acts of worship and everything else, some have unintentionally demolished the very foundation of Christian living. They have destroyed the possibility of the very principle for which they are contending. Has this generation of the church been deceived in the name of the worship and service of God? Is it a coincidence that Sabbath-keeping has declined rapidly at the same time that the church has made an enormous shift in her views of corporate worship and her relation to this present world? Does this not run the risk of promoting the kind of "religious" worldliness described above? May the Sabbath help show us that we are spiritually out of shape.

CHAPTER SIX

What Is Missing?

Something is evidently missing in the way many approach the Christian life today. It is easy to assert that believers must live to the glory of God in every aspect of life. It is even easier to use this principle to justify whatever we are doing, so long as it is not expressly forbidden in Scripture. There are, however, pitfalls on every side. Some Christians abuse the (true) idea that all of life should be lived to God's glory, in order to justify worldliness (or earthly mindedness) without realizing it. Other Christians have simply not given enough thought to Christian living. Overall, what seems to be missing is, simultaneously, a practical grasp of how dangerous "this present evil age" can be, as well as a positive understanding of how to live life before the face of God. What is missing in our Christianity is further highlighted by the manner in which the church is "shamed" by the piety that God required of Israel in the Old Testament. These things point to the fact that genuine Sabbath-keeping is often one of the best preservatives against hypocrisy in the church.

Two Vital Principles

The Present Evil Age

In order to steer clear of worldliness, there are two important questions to ask: What is the relationship of Christians to this world as in its current condition, and what principles ought to characterize their lives in this world? The apostle John answered the first question: "We know that we are of God, and the whole world lieth in wickedness [i.e., the wicked one]" (1 John 5:19). The answer to the second question is summarized in Colossians 3: "If ye then be risen with Christ, seek those things which are above where Christ sitteth on the right hand of God. Set your affection [literally, mind] on things above, not on things on the earth" (Col. 3:1–2). The answers to these two questions both supplement and complement each other. The first teaches us how we are to regard this world, and the second teaches us how we should live in this world in light of these things.

The "wicked one" has no authority in himself. God rules and reigns over all. Yet the Scriptures tell us unequivocally that the days in which we live are evil (Eph. 5:16), that Satan is in some sense "the god of this world" (2 Cor. 4:4), and that both the rulers and people of the earth rage against the Lord and against His Christ (Ps. 2:1–3). Christians have become far too trusting of this present world. We act as though it is easy to use the things of this world without misusing them (1 Cor. 7:31), and that it is a simple task to do all things to the glory of God, "who giveth us richly all things to enjoy" (1 Tim. 6:17). By contrast, Owen warned, "Earthly enjoyments enlarge men's earthly desires, and the love of them grows with their income."[1] This is not to say that you should not enjoy the good things of this life and that the blessing of God cannot accompany them. In whatever you do, whether you eat or drink, you must do all things to the glory of God (1 Cor. 10:31), but you must recognize that this is not an easy task and that the "ruler of this world" is seeking to destroy and devour you. The present life is characterized by darkness (John 1:5). The entertainments and pleasures of this life are not neutral, and you must not treat them as such. The people presenting "the world" to you on television, in movies, and through other media will not retain God in their thinking (Rom. 1:28). They are not for Christ, but they are against Him. You must not adopt what they view as "normal" because it is acceptable in society at large. "Thou shalt not follow a multitude to do evil" (Ex. 23:2). This is why you must not love the world or the things in the world; the world is in opposition to your God.

---

1. Owen, "Grace and Duty," 331.

This does not mean that Christians cannot legitimately enjoy "worldly" pleasures, such as movies or sports. It does, however, place two limitations upon you. You must be wary and suspicious of what is inherently sinful becoming acceptable and normal without your notice. You must also be aware that indulging in activities that are otherwise "innocent" often satisfies the unbelieving world. It does not follow that because an activity is *lawful* it is invariably *safe*. The world does not encourage a moderate use of the things of the world, and when it speaks of moderation it often has nothing to do with the standards set forth in Scripture. The problem is things that are harmless in themselves become dangerous when they do not have respect to God or become a dominant part of life. For example, a believer may enjoy a football game as an enjoyable way to rest from the hectic activities of life. Yet he may soon tell himself that since watching football is lawful entertainment, he should be able to watch it as often as he likes. After all, many other men do the same and it is a harmless recreation. Soon his love for "the game" may come in conflict with some of his other duties, and he neglects his duty instead of his sport. The fact that his enjoyment of a game has turned into worldliness and idolatry is particularly uncovered when his football game comes into conflict with God's worship. At this point, the man will either determine that he must watch his game regardless of the conflict of interests, or skip the game and struggle to worship because his heart is with football rather than with his Lord. In either case, Satan has won. Have you forgotten that you may lose sight of Christ and of heaven by an inordinate love for the lawful activities of this life? Satan does not have to tempt you to gross sins such as atheism, adultery, murder, or prodigal living. If he merely convinces you that you are safe as long as you engage in activities you know are lawful, he has achieved his purpose in you.[2]

---

2. C. S. Lewis has illustrated the subtlety of this temptation as only he was able to do. In the *Screwtape Letters*, the older experienced demon counsels his younger counterpart not to waste his time trying to tempt a man into "big" sins, but simply to present him with every distraction the world has to offer. He says, "Murder is no better than cards if cards can do the trick. Indeed, the

Some Characteristics of Godly Living

In order to use this world properly, the believer must walk upon the earth with his eyes lifted up to heaven. Christians are those who use the things of this life with their hopes set upon heaven and with heaven in view. The manner in which the gospel should transform the *speech* of believers illustrates this well. I have argued in the previous chapter that our speech on the Sabbath should consist of conversation directed to promote the worship of God and the edification of others. There ought to be a seriousness and gravity that hovers about the Christian's life and speech in general. The speech of believers should be carried out in light of eternal realities. For this reason, our speech should always have a purpose. We should take seriously the command given in Ephesians 4:29: "Let no corrupt communication proceed out of your mouth, but that which is good for the use of edifying, that it may minister grace unto the hearers." D. Martyn Lloyd-Jones wrote concerning our speech:

> There must be some purpose in it, some point in it, some value in it. We are not to chatter away the time and talk about nothing. Oh! the hours we have all wasted in life in sheer idle talk and chatter and gossip, and all to no value! The Christian must turn from this. He need not always of necessity talk of religion, but whenever he speaks there must always be some point and some value in it. It must always be good, it must always be clean, it must always in some sense or another be edifying, so that people may say at the end, It was a good thing to have spent some time with that man or woman, I feel better for having done so. I am almost tempted to say that one of the main differences between pagan and Christian conversation is that Christian conversation is always intelligent and the other is not.[3]

---

safest road to hell is the gradual one—the gentle slope, soft underfoot, without sudden turnings, without milestones, without signposts." C. S. Lewis, *The Screwtape Letters* (New York: Touchstone, 1961), 54.

3. D. Martyn Lloyd-Jones, *Darkness and Light* (Grand Rapids: Eerdmans, 1982), 260.

The transformation that Christ brings to our lives by the power of His Spirit means that although our conversation will not always have respect to spiritual things, it will always have a spiritual purpose, with an aim to honor God and edify the person to whom we are speaking. The speech that should characterize Sabbath-keeping is really not so different. The only difference is that in addition to including spiritual aims in every conversation, we must be eager to include spiritual objects in our conversation. If you converse in this manner throughout the week, should not the Sabbath be a natural transition for you? This is like two people, who have been assuming and implying a topic in a conversation, breathing a sigh of relief when things are finally "out in the open" and they can speak plainly and directly. The Sabbath, above all other days, is the day in which the Christian should feel the most "at home" in this present life.

It is too often that on the Sabbath, we fill our speech with such things as are unbecoming of Christians at all times. It is not that the things themselves are wrong, but rather the proportion of attention we direct toward them and falling short of an edifying purpose in our speech. William Sprague's *Lectures on Revival* provide a well-needed corrective to the manner in which the modern church views the Christian life. Sprague described the conversation of worldly men in this manner: "They are quite absorbed with the things that are seen and temporal. Their conversation is not in heaven. It breathes not the spirit of heaven. It does not relate to the enjoyments of heaven, or the means of reaching those enjoyments. The world takes knowledge of them, not that they have been with Jesus, but that, like themselves, they love to grovel amidst things below."[4] Far from presenting an unhealthy view of this life, this is the only proper response to the spiritual realities that should be determinative for the believer's life.

When we honestly search ourselves, do we delight more in conversing about earthly things than about heavenly things? Mary

---

4. William B. Sprague, *Lectures on Revival of Religion* (Edinburgh: Banner of Truth, 2008), 51.

Winslow, the mother of Octavius Winslow, once recounted to one of her sons how she had been filled with guilt and grief after discovering that she had gone an entire hour in conversation without mentioning "the precious Savior." This was on a weekday and not on the Sabbath![5] Burroughs argued that no mature believer in Christ should ever leave the presence of another believer without discussing the things of the Lord. To do so would be like an Englishman in a foreign country meeting another Englishman there and not asking him how things were going back at home.[6] We who have such a glorious hope should have no need to be told that we must speak in this manner. Out of the overflow of the heart the mouth speaks (Luke 6:45). The Sabbath aside, how often do we consider whether or not our speech is imparting grace to those who hear us (Eph. 4:29)? Do we consciously strive to speak nothing apart from that which is necessary for edification? Remember that it was the Lord Jesus Christ who said, "By thy words thou shalt be justified, and by thy words thou shalt be condemned" (Matt. 12:37).

The two most disputed points of Sabbath-keeping are recreation and speech. It is telling that these same two areas demonstrate so many of the deficiencies in modern views of Christian living. Perhaps our primary problem is not our thoughts, words, and works about our worldly employments and recreations on the Sabbath, but that we are too consumed with these on the other six days of the week. Our American culture is obsessed with recreation and entertainment. We can discuss business or sports, but we cannot discuss religion. Whatever else we may do, we act as though we cannot sacrifice our recreation and entertainment. Do we not inculcate this into our children? Our culture virtually mandates that our children must be involved in every sport possible. Do we not teach our children that practicing for sports is more important than the weekly prayer meeting when we skip it for the sake of soccer practice? Do we not teach

---

5. Octavius Winslow, *Life in Jesus: A Memoir of Mrs. Mary Winslow* (London: Paternoster Row, 1890; repr., Morgan, Pa.: Soli Deo Gloria, 1993), 184.

6. Burroughs, *Earthly Mindedness*, 121.

them that watching the "big game" is more momentous and exciting than entering into the presence of the God before whom the angels shield their faces (Isa. 6:2), when we come to church for corporate worship? Are they becoming skilled in conversing about this world, but unskilled in the word of righteousness because our own conversation is filled with worldly things more than the things of the Lord? Since we are seeing the astonishing worldliness of the rising generation and have a growing concern for the young people in the church, let us often ask the sobering questions: "Are our children departing from the faith? Or are they simply becoming just like us?"

Sabbath-keeping ought to be the natural expression of the life of a person who is heavenly minded. It should be the culmination and high point of every week. A sacred day consecrated to the worship of God should be what the Christian looks forward to most every week. The Sabbath ought to be the day on which believers feel most alive and most clearly express their faith in Christ. It is the epitome of Christian living. Heavenly minded people should live and speak in such a manner that causes them to long for the Sabbath day every week. The way they keep the Sabbath should have this effect upon other people as well. The Sabbath, in turn, will help them become more heavenly minded the next week, and long even more for the next Sabbath. This cycle should continue until believers one day enter the eternal Sabbath in glory. This is why the Westminster divines asserted that the Sabbath helps equip men and women to keep all of the commandments of God better throughout the rest of the week (Larger Catechism 121).

Shamed by Israel

Although the fact of worldliness is exposed by the widespread neglect of the Sabbath, there is another factor that highlights the weakness of the church in this area. Greater privileges should provide greater cause for gratitude and thankfulness. In terms of our relationship to God, this thankfulness is expressed by offering Him the worship due His name. One fact that serves to expose our worldly nakedness and shame is what little emphasis we place upon corporate worship in comparison to the saints of the Old Testament. The role that "Sabbaths" as days of worship held in the religious life of Israel sets this in painful relief. It is hard to deny that believers in Christ have far greater advantages and blessings, as well as far more glorious causes for praise and worship, than Old Testament Israel. We have better promises than they had (Heb. 8:6), and we look back with clarity upon the finished work of Christ, which they looked forward to in obscurity. However, when it comes to expressing thanksgiving and gratitude for the gospel through worship, is the modern church put to shame by ancient Israel?

We have already seen in chapter 4 that the Sabbath was the pattern after which every religious day of observance in the Old Testament was modeled. In Leviticus 16 and 23, each of the major feasts in the Jewish year was called a "Sabbath" and included a "holy convocation" to the Lord. This meant that Old Testament believers at times observed several "Sabbaths" in one week. The seventh month of the Jewish calendar illustrates this point. During this month, the children of Israel observed the Feast of Trumpets, the Day of Atonement, and the Feast of Tabernacles (Num. 29). The first day of the month marked the Feast of Trumpets (vv. 1–6). On this day, work was forbidden so that the people could observe a "holy convocation" and come together for the prescribed sacrifices. This cessation from labor was not for idleness or recreation, but for the purpose of worshiping God. Let us suppose then that the regular weekly Sabbath occurred on the seventh day of this month. This would mean that in the first week of the month, Israel would have sanctified two Sabbaths to the Lord.

On the tenth day of the month, they observed another "holy convocation" (v. 7), or "Sabbath" (Lev. 16:31), which was the Day of Atonement. On this day, rather than feasting, God commanded the people to "afflict" their souls as they humbled themselves for the atonement of their sins.[7] This was only three days after the weekly

7. For the New Testament Sabbath, although it celebrates the redemption purchased by Christ, the distinctive note is that of the resurrection

Sabbath. Since the first weekly Sabbath occurred on the seventh day of the month, the next one occurred on the fourteenth day of the month, only four days after the Day of Atonement. Israel had already set apart four entire days for worship in two weeks. On the fifteenth day of the month, the Feast of Tabernacles began (Num. 29:12). Including the weekly Sabbath, this required two Sabbaths in a row. The feast concluded on the eighth day by the Israelites observing another Sabbath to the Lord (v. 35). The last day of the feast was the twenty-fifth day of the month. The weekly Sabbath was observed on the twenty-first day of the month. Then the last Sabbath in the seventh month was observed on the twenty-eighth day. In addition to these days set apart *entirely* for worship, the other six days of the Feast of Tabernacles required acts of worship above and beyond the daily temple sacrifices.

In an ordinary month, we observe the Lord's Day four times; occasionally, we observe it five times. In the seventh month of the year, Israel observed at least eight Sabbaths, along with other increased acts of corporate worship. In the model presented above, sometimes God's people could have observed three Sabbaths in a seven-day period. We fail miserably to keep one day out of seven in its most basic form by ceasing from our labors, let alone keeping it holy to the Lord as a day of worship. Imagine keeping three Sabbaths in one week. We justify our Sabbath-breaking once a week by arguing that it is impossible for us to get along in life and to provide for our families without breaking the Sabbath now and then, yet God still provided for the families of Israel when they kept eight or nine Sabbaths in a month. You may ask how this is possible in light of work obligations, yet is this not exactly what you do when you prepare for a family vacation? When you prepare to take eight days off of work to spend with your family, you do not ask, "How is this

and Christ's victory over death. For this reason, the example of the Day of Atonement does not set a precedent for fasting upon the Lord's Day. Both are Sabbath days of rest for the purpose of worship, but the Sabbath under the New Testament should never be a day of grief. This would be like attending a wedding with the disposition appropriate to a funeral.

possible?" You simply plan ahead. If we can plan ahead for family vacations and can escape work for two weeks without the economic security of our families collapsing, then can we not plan ahead for one "spiritual vacation" per week on the Sabbath day?

It is a great tragedy that though we have the greatest reasons to worship and serve the triune God, the Old Testament saints should outdo us in corporate worship. We struggle to make it to at least one service every Lord's Day, while at times Israel set aside several days of one week for worship exclusively. Should those who attended the earthly sanctuary be heavenly minded, while those who approach the heavenly sanctuary through Christ are earthly minded? Israel could not bear to look upon the glory of the face of Moses when he came from the presence of God. For this reason, Moses wore a veil over his face to shield the people from the radiant reflection of the glory of Jehovah (Ex. 34:33–35; 2 Cor. 3:13). Under the gospel, we behold the glory of God in the face of Jesus Christ (2 Cor. 3:18, 4:6). We read the Old Testament with unveiled eyes, and we see wonders that believers under the old covenant scarcely dreamed of. Yet we are often outdone by the worship practices of God's ancient people. We struggle to set apart one day out of seven to the worship and service of God exclusively when God often required much more than this from the nation of Israel.

This does not mean we should begin multiplying days dedicated to the worship and glory of God. It is sufficient if we observe the one day of worship God has already provided for us. Doing this shall put us in a more spiritual frame of mind throughout the week. Self-conscious Sabbath-keeping makes doing everything else to the glory of God a natural reflection of our lives. Many believers marvel that Jesus was often able to spend entire nights in communion with His Father in prayer. How could we even think of setting our minds upon a task such as prayer for such a length of time? In case the example of Jesus seems too high and unrealistic, I knew a group of Korean Christians in California who used to come together after work every Friday evening to spend the entire night in prayer together. Not only is this fact itself remarkable, but the attendance at this prayer meeting was almost identical to their Sunday morning worship services. I am not suggesting we should begin spending all night in prayer once a week. Yet even Israel spent more time in extended and intense acts of spiritual worship than most believers do today. Dismissing your thoughts, words, and works about your worldly employments and recreations for twenty-four hours once a week will make it easier for you to avoid being consumed by them the rest of the time. This will make living life before the face of God more natural. On a personal note, I found that after my first year of enjoying the Sabbath as a day of worship, laying aside everything other than the hope of heaven, it became less difficult to keep God in my thoughts the rest of the week. Brethren, let us not be shamed by Israel.

Conclusions

We live in a time in which the church closely resembles the surrounding culture. The Westminster position on Sabbath-keeping cannot survive in a worldly church and, in many respects, it has not. It is telling that at the present time, so few churches possess a rich heritage of love for the Sabbath as a day of worship and thus retain this position in doctrine or in practice. Sabbath-keeping either causes the church to flee from worldliness, or worldliness causes the church to abandon the Sabbath. It appears the latter has happened on a large scale.

Perhaps the greatest indicator of our worldliness is our aversion to cast off our thoughts, words, and works about our worldly employments and recreations in order to spend a day of communion with the Trinity. Does this not indicate how little we treasure communion with God? When you are called to enjoy communion with God and His people for an entire day, without the distractions of work or recreation, should your hearts not long delight in such a day? It is one thing to say you do not believe that God binds you to keep the Sabbath in this manner, but when you react against the very idea as strict and legalistic, how can this be anything less than a sign of worldliness and an insult to the Father, Son, and Holy Spirit?

There can be only three explanations for this kind of reaction. First, our perception of the relationship between the law and the gospel has become distorted (see chapter 9). Second, although we love the Lord Jesus Christ, we have to some degree loved this world and the things of the world more than worship and communion with our Savior. Third and far more sobering, our aversion to the idea of a day of worship may indicate that we are enemies of the cross of Christ when we set our minds upon earthly things. I have met many true children of God who do not believe they should keep the Sabbath in the manner in which I am convinced they should. However, I have met some professing the name of the Lord Jesus Christ who act as though one day of nothing but worship would be the most dreadful thing in the world. They do not simply disagree over Sabbath-keeping; they respond to it adversely. Should you not search out your own hearts? Are you willing to set aside the toil and entertainments of this world for a little while in order to worship your Creator? I know few people who do not desire to go to heaven. Many even profess that they hope to get there by faith in Jesus Christ and in His death and resurrection. Yet the faith of many is practical only for the life to come and has no effect on the present time. Worship is the focus of heaven. Worship is the primary joy of heaven. Does it speak well of the state of your heart if the day designed to resemble heaven on earth most closely is repulsive to you?

Keeping the Sabbath as a day of worship will either help *prevent* hypocrisy in religion or it will help *expose* it. Observing the Sabbath as a day of worship to the Lord must either begin killing the worldliness dwelling in the hearts of God's people, or it will uncover it to an extent they have never known before. With the blessing of God, Sabbath-keeping will help you overcome your love for the world and the things in the world. Or it may show that you are altogether consumed by the world, in which case the love of the Father is not in you (1 John 2:17). If we are honest with ourselves, does not the Sabbath show us how little we set our minds on things above where Christ is seated at the right hand of the Father (Col. 3:2)? It is our duty to be spiritually minded every day in all that we do. This is true with respect to our "worldly" employments and recreations as well. On the Sabbath, we are simply called to be consumed with heavenly glories, communion with God, and religious worship more directly than on other days. What person, who genuinely knows what it is to be redeemed by such a glorious Savior and has such hope in Him, could call this duty a burden? Our hope in Christ should give us a bias in favor of keeping one day of seven holy to the Lord. We should long that every day were a Sabbath for the worship of God. Do we not profess this in some measure when we say that our citizenship is in heaven, from which we eagerly await the Savior (Phil. 3:20)?

Perhaps the Westminster doctrine of the Sabbath is so painful to many because it places a firm finger on a besetting sin that mars the entirety of their Christian lives. If this book does not change your position on Sabbath-keeping, then I at least implore you to examine your Christian life as a whole! If you discover yourself to be hypocritical in your love to Christ, repent of your wickedness and pray God that the thought of your heart may be forgiven you (Acts 8:22). If you are in Christ, see whether you have undervalued the worship of the God who loved you and gave Himself for you, and whether you have loved the world too greatly. If Sabbath-breaking points to the fact that we are out of shape spiritually, then Sabbath-keeping provides the exercise needed to train us to run the race set before us with endurance.

CHAPTER SEVEN

The Reformed
Application of the Law

Not all corrective lenses help all people see clearly. A prescription that helps one person see may blur the vision of another. The truths of Scripture are similar in some respects. Biblical truths do not change whether people understand them properly or not; yet one person may come to understand what the Scriptures say on a subject through one set of arguments, while someone else finds an entirely different set of arguments convincing. Isaiah 58:13–14 is all that is needed to convince some people that "the Sabbath is to be sanctified by a holy resting all that day, even from such worldly employments and recreations as are lawful on other days; and spending the whole time in the public and private exercises of God's worship, except so much as is to be taken up in the works of necessity and mercy" (Westminster Shorter Catechism, 60–61). Even though some do not believe that Isaiah 58 supports the catechism definition, however, it is possible to come to the same conclusion from other biblical principles.

The purpose of this chapter is to demonstrate that the principles of Sabbath-keeping set forth in the Westminster Standards are demanded by the principles upon which Jesus and His apostles interpreted and applied the law of God. These principles demonstrate that the entire Sabbath should be set apart for the purposes of public and private worship in thought, word, and deed. The general characteristics of the law of God combined with the New Testament application of the sixth commandment will serve as a "template" for interpreting the fourth commandment. This approach to the principles of Sabbath-keeping will help clarify the issue by placing

Sabbath-keeping within the broader context of the biblical and Reformed model of the attitude those who love the Lord Jesus Christ should have toward the law of God.

Biblical Rules for Interpreting the Law

General Considerations

There are both general and specific considerations that are important in order to interpret the law of God properly.[1] Generally speaking, the law of God reflects the character of God Himself. The law is holy, just, and good (Rom. 7:12). It is a mirror that reveals the glory of God and of Jesus Christ, who fulfilled the righteous requirement of the law for His people (Rom. 8:3–4). When we sin against the law, we do not sin against an impersonal list of abstract principles; we sin against the triune God personally by violating the reflection of His holy character. Loving the law of God and loving God are inseparable. This is a vital point because it means that the moral law is an eternal and immutable standard. Whoever is indifferent to the law of God is indifferent to the God of the law. Most people do not realize that they are sinners and that their carnal or unconverted minds are at enmity with God (Rom. 8:7) until they are confronted with the law of God.[2] To despise God's law is to despise God. Moreover, Jesus Christ was born of a woman and made under the law so that He might redeem those who were under the curse of the law (Gal. 4:4–5). The law not only reflects God as Creator, but it also reflects the God who took on human flesh and obeyed the law on behalf of His chosen people. As Walter Chantry observes, "The life of our Lord Jesus Christ was the first biographical inscription of the Moral

---

1. For an excellent treatment of the interpretation of the law, see the introductory chapters of Plumer, *Law of God*. I am greatly indebted to Larger Catechism Question 99 for the general approach of this chapter.

2. Jonathan Edwards wrote, "The strictness of God's law is a principle cause of man's enmity against him." Jonathan Edwards, "Men Naturally God's Enemies," in *The Works of Jonathan Edwards* (repr., Edinburgh: Banner of Truth, 1997), 2:133.

Law."[3] Those who love the Father because Christ first loved them and gave Himself for them cannot but love His law, since the law bears the imprint and image of the God and Savior whom they love.

The fact that the law mirrors the character of God also means that the law of the Lord is as perfect as the Lord of the law (Ps. 19:7). God demands allegiance from man in every respect: in body, in soul, and in every faculty of both. This means that the law of God, as summarized in the Ten Commandments (Deut. 5:22), is a *perfect* standard for righteousness. There is no aspect of life—whether regarding outward actions, words, and gestures, or "the understanding, will, affections, and all other powers of the soul" (Larger Catechism 99.2)—that the law of God does not address. This is why the psalmist, meditating on the nature of the law of God, wrote, "I have seen an end of all perfection: but thy commandment is exceeding broad" (Ps. 119:96). No one shall ever be able to say in this life that he has ceased from sin (1 Kings 8:46; Prov. 20:9; Eccl. 7:20; 1 John 1:8–10). This applies even to those redeemed from the power of sin by Jesus Christ. Until believers enter into the presence of the Lord in heaven, the holy and perfect law of God is the path that has been paved for them to express their love to God through Jesus Christ. The triune God has no standard other than His own holy character, which is reflected by His law. The rule for God's children is that they must be imitators of God (Eph. 5:1). Though Christians are neither condemned nor justified by the law, and though they keep it imperfectly at best, by definition they delight in the law of God according to the inward man (Rom. 7:22). The law of God is an inflexible standard of righteousness, and the implications of the commandments of God are far reaching. Additionally, because Christ has taken away the condemnation of the law, the law of God is the "perfect law of liberty" (James 1:25). It has become "the law of Christ" (Rom. 3:30).

---

3. Walter Chantry, *God's Righteous Kingdom* (Edinburgh: Banner of Truth, 1980), 78.

A Specific Example

In general, the commandments of God reflect the character of the
God who gave them, and the obedience demanded by those commandments reaches man's inmost being as well as all of his actions.
This has important implications for understanding and applying each commandment in particular. The best place to learn how
to understand and apply the commandments of God is from the
teaching and example of Jesus Christ and His apostles. Jesus Christ
gave a useful pattern for interpreting and applying the Ten Commandments in His exposition of the sixth commandment: "Thou
shalt not kill," literally, murder (Ex. 20:13).[4] Each commandment is
designed to serve as a "subject heading" or category. As the Westminster Larger Catechism summarizes: "Under one sin or duty, all
of the same kind are forbidden or commanded; together with all
the causes, means, occasions, and appearances thereof, and provo-
cations thereunto" (Larger Catechism, 99.6). For this reason, Jesus
contradicted the traditional Jewish interpretation of the sixth commandment, which relegated its observance to the outward act of
murder (Matt. 5:21). Jesus confronted this interpretation by adding
several qualifications. First, He demonstrated that this commandment forbade unjustified anger in the *heart* as much as murder
by the hand: "But I say to you, That whosoever is angry with his
brother without a cause shall be in danger of the judgment" (v. 22).
In addition to the heart, the triune God regards our *speech* in this
commandment. As Jesus added, "And whosoever shall say to his
brother, Raca, shall be in danger of the council: but whosoever shall
say, Thou fool, shall be in danger of hell fire" (v. 22b).

The significance of the next scenario to which Jesus applied the
sixth commandment may not be immediately apparent. In verses
23–24, He said, "Therefore if thou bring thy gift to the altar and there

---

4. My purpose in this chapter is not to give a full defense of the Reformed
view of the law (since space does not permit), but rather to establish principles
to be used in interpreting the fourth commandment. For the most part, I can
only identity and describe them. For a detailed and powerful exposition of the
principles set forth here, see Murray, *Principles of Conduct*, 157–67.

rememberest that thy brother hath ought against thee; leave there thy gift before the altar, and go thy way; first be reconciled to thy brother, and then come and offer thy gift." The word "therefore" demonstrates that not only are these verses *connected* with the preceding teaching about the sixth commandment, but they are also legitimately *concluded* from that teaching.[5] In other words, in order to keep the sixth commandment, we must be reconciled with our brother. What is in view here is a man going to the temple with his gift to worship God. At the very foot of the altar, he remembers that he has a brother who holds something against him. Reconciliation with his brother is so urgent that the man must temporarily delay worship and be reconciled to his brother first. The text does not say whether or not the brother's complaint is legitimate; apparently it does not matter. The implication of these verses is that the sixth commandment demands appropriate action toward others when *they* violate the commandment. Jesus did not teach anything new or surprising here. This concern had already been expressed in the Old Testament: "Deliver those who are drawn towards death, and hold back those stumbling to the slaughter. If you say, 'surely we did not know this,' does not he who weighs the hearts consider it? He who keeps your soul, does he not know it? And will he not render to each man according to his deeds?" (Prov. 24:11–12, my translation). This example reveals that it is not good enough to be concerned with keeping the commandments of God without respect to how one's neighbor keeps them. The negative commandment, "Thou shalt not kill," implies the positive requirement to preserve the lives of others and to do all in our power to prevent anything that might cause them harm.

Building upon these principles, the Westminster Shorter Catechism summarizes the teaching of Scripture on the sixth commandment by stating that this commandment requires "all lawful endeavors to preserve our own life, and the life of others," and that it forbids "the taking away of our own life, or the life of our neighbor unjustly, or whatsoever tendeth thereunto" (Q. 68–69).

---

5. Murray, *Principles of Conduct*, 162.

Those tempted to object that this conclusion stretches the intent of the commandment must recognize that Jesus Christ expected His contemporaries to apply the law by virtue of these principles. Outward acts of murder represent the highest violation of the sixth commandment. Unjustified anger is murder in the heart because it is out of the heart that murders, adulteries, and other abominable crimes proceed (Matt. 15:19). Malicious speech harms a neighbor and belongs to the same genre. That the positive duty of the commandment is to pursue whatever tends to preserve the lives of others is assumed by the fact that believers must seek not to encourage the sins of others against the sixth commandment, even when it involves sins of the heart. James accused some of violating the sixth commandment by showing favoritism to the rich and despising the poor (James 2:5–13). These are only a few examples of how to keep or break one commandment by varying degrees. Truly the commandments are exceedingly broad. Jesus' use of the sixth commandment treats the Ten Commandments as a system of classification, under which every application of the law of God should be placed. As Calvin noted, "In each commandment we must investigate what it is concerned with; then we must seek out its purpose."[6]

Plugging the Fourth Commandment into the Equation

If Jesus and His inspired apostles provide a model for applying the law of God (and if the church cannot appeal to their example, to what example can she appeal?), then the fourth commandment must be understood and applied in harmony with this model. First, the Sabbath is both positive and negative in scope; it contains requirements as well as prohibitions. Second, the Sabbath must be observed and can be broken by outward actions in respect both to requirements and to prohibitions. Third, the Sabbath must be observed and can be broken in the heart. Fourth, the Sabbath must be observed and can

---

6. John Calvin, *Institutes of the Christian Religion*, trans. Ford Lewis Battles, ed. John T. McNeill (Philadelphia: Westminster Press, 1960), 2.8.8.

be broken through speech. Fifth, the Sabbath must be observed and can be broken by actions toward other people. By combining the first two of these categories, I will summarize the biblical principles of Sabbath-keeping in the next four sections.

What Are the Basic Commands and Prohibitions
of the Fourth Commandment?

The first observation about the fourth commandment is that it is primarily concerned with direct acts of love toward the triune God. It is not that the first four commandments have nothing to do with man's relation to his neighbor, but rather that these four commandments deal more directly with man's relationship with God. No one can keep the Sabbath, therefore, unless he comes to the Father, through Jesus Christ, by the Holy Spirit (Eph. 2:18). He will then exercise that love by keeping the Sabbath accordingly. This is not the same as simply acknowledging God in every aspect of the daily business of life. In that sense, the saints can love God by loving their neighbors and by going to work. The first four commandments address the manner in which we must love God in and of Himself. This is the foundation of our relationship to anyone or anything else in the world. The requirements of the fourth commandment accentuate this fact clearly.

It has become common to treat rest or cessation from labor as the positive and summary requirement of the fourth commandment.[7] However, "in it thou shalt not do any work," is the *prohibition* of the fourth commandment, not the *requirement* of the commandment. The summary requirement is, "Remember the Sabbath day *to keep it holy.*"[8] "In it thou shalt not do any work," is a prohibition added by God as a necessary prerequisite to keeping the day *holy*. No one can love a man unless he first stops hating him in his heart. Similarly,

---

7. For example, see Robert Vasholz, *Leviticus: A Mentor Commentary* (Fearn, U.K.: Christian Focus Publications, 2007), 284: "The sole goal of the weekly Sabbath is rest."

8. See chapter 2 for more detail on this point.

no one is able to keep the Sabbath until he first ceases from ordinary labor. Thomas Shepard, who founded Harvard University, wrote:

> The word Sabbath properly signifies, not common, but *sacred* or *holy* rest. The Lord, therefore, enjoins this rest from labor upon this day, not so much for the rest's sake, but because it is a medium, or means of that holiness which the Lord requires upon this day; otherwise the Sabbath is a day of idleness, not of holiness; our cattle rest but a common rest from labor as well as we; and therefore it is man's sin and shame if he improve the day no better than the beasts that perish.[9]

The word order in the title of John Owen's work on the Sabbath reflects this in a significant manner. The abbreviated title is "A Day of Sacred Rest," as opposed to "A Sacred Day of Rest."[10] The Sabbath is not a sacred day that is observed by resting. The Sabbath is a day on which the characteristic or quality of the rest is sacred.

Any interpretation of the fourth commandment that makes cessation from labor the sum and substance of the commandment is not in harmony with Jesus' manner of applying the Decalogue. No commandment of God contains a prohibition only. If a requirement is not stated in any commandment, it is always implied. Prohibiting labor cannot stand by itself without a corresponding positive requirement. Those who interpret the fourth commandment purely in terms of avoiding weekly employments end up with a mutilated half-Sabbath. This is like a man who clears land to build a house and thinks his work is done, when he has not yet laid the foundation. The outward actions required by the fourth commandment are attending the public and private exercises of God's worship. People cannot keep the Sabbath unless they "keep it holy." The positive requirements of the Ten Commandments must always govern our understanding of the prohibitions, not vice versa. The only reason

9. Thomas Shepard, *Theses Sabbaticae* (1649; repr., Dahlonega, Ga.: Crown Rights Book Company, 2002), 254.

10. Owen, "Day of Sacred Rest," 263–460. This is an outstanding and powerfully argued work that is still relevant today.

why labor, or any other activity, is prohibited on the Sabbath is because it contradicts the positive purposes of the day. Labor is the greatest example of what is prohibited in the fourth commandment, but labor is not the only thing prohibited in the fourth commandment. The command to keep the Sabbath day holy excludes "worldly recreations" as much as "worldly employments," because the holiness of the day does not consist in recreations. This does not mean that recreation cannot be "holy" on other days in the broad sense of the term, but the holiness required in keeping the Sabbath requires setting the day apart from common uses to holy uses. If we must observe a prohibition and a requirement in the sixth commandment, then we must observe a prohibition and a requirement in the fourth commandment. "Rest" and cessation from labor are synonymous expressions. If we rest on the Sabbath day, then we have obeyed part of the prohibition of the commandment—but how do we "keep it holy?"

How Should Christians Observe the Fourth Commandment in Their Hearts?

Just as the sixth commandment is violated by unjustified anger in the heart, so the Sabbath can be violated in the heart. The Sabbath must be sanctified in the heart by calling it a delight (Isa. 58:13), through loving the day and the activities of the day. For believers, the highest delight of the Sabbath should be celebrating the resurrection of the Lord Jesus Christ, who inaugurated the New Testament Sabbath on the day He rose from the dead. What is more conducive to worship and joy? If the duties of the day are burdensome, and Christians cannot wait until the Sabbath is over, they are guilty of Sabbath-breaking. In the days of the prophet Amos, the Israelites committed this sin when they said, "When will the new moon be gone, that we may sell corn? and the sabbath, that we may set forth [i.e., trade] wheat?" (Amos 8:5). If people cannot wait for the Sabbath to be over because they prefer other activities, then they are violating the Sabbath day. Should we not *love* the one day that is specially designed for worshiping our God and Redeemer? Sadly, few are willing to give much attention to the disposition of their hearts in their Sabbath-keeping. If our hearts do not rest upon the glory of God and His worship, then the praise of our mouths on the Lord's Day has become forced hypocrisy. Like the depiction of the "worshiping" Jews in the last book of the Old Testament, we effectually say, "Behold, what a weariness is it!" (Mal. 1:13). Even from the standpoint of ceasing from weekly labors, can we genuinely say we are resting from our labor on the Sabbath when we do so only with our bodies and not our hearts? If we must keep the sixth commandment in our hearts, then we must also keep the fourth commandment in our hearts.

How Should Christians Observe the Fourth Commandment in Their Speech?

We keep the Sabbath in our hearts and outward actions, but we also keep it with our words. The more we grow to love the Sabbath day and its purposes, the more naturally this will come to us. If we occupy our time with worshiping the triune God in the corporate assembly, in the family, and in private, as well as with edifying conversation with His people, our speech will correspond to what is in our hearts. We will rejoice that we have nothing else to concern us on the Lord's Day. But our speech often betrays us. If we are not at work on Sunday, attending church and being with our brethren in Christ, yet we speak predominantly about what is happening at the office or about our favorite sporting events, how can our hearts be in our Sabbath-keeping? If your body is where it should be on the Sabbath but your mind and mouth travel abroad, your bodily presence is more like a corpse than a living, worshiping soul. On the contrary, the speech of God's people on the Sabbath should be filled with the glories of the triune God and His work of redemption in Christ.

Some things that are lawful and appropriate topics of conversation on other days become signs of apathy and disregard for God's glorious presence on the Lord's Day. If spiritual conversation proves difficult even for genuine Christians, the Sabbath is the best occasion for them to grow in this area. If you object that you struggle with material for conversation, then consider what you can glean from the preaching of the Word in corporate worship. Is it not part of our calling as believers to seek the profit of others in all that we say and do? If we must keep the sixth commandment in our speech, then we must keep the fourth commandment in our speech.

How Does our Sabbath-Keeping Relate to Other People?
In what respect must we exercise care and concern for others in their Sabbath-keeping? If *all people* must keep the Sabbath, then we must not encourage our neighbors to violate the Sabbath.[11] According to Jesus, if a brother has something against you, you must do all within your power to be reconciled to him so that neither of you are guilty of violating the commandment not to murder. In a similar manner, if your neighbor is working on the Sabbath, the *least* you can do out of love for his soul is to avoid giving him your business. If you hire others to break the commandments of God for you, you have still broken them. If you hire someone to kill another person, you are guilty of murder. If you hire someone to steal something for you, you are guilty of theft. If you bribe someone to act as a false witness in a courtroom, you are guilty of perjury. Scripture alone does not require the principle of keeping the law in relation to others. Even the laws of modern secular society recognize that this is a necessary moral implication of law. Is it not strange when the church does not apply this to Sabbath-keeping? Is it not strange when Christians do not hesitate to hire pilots and flight attendants to break the Sabbath for them? Is it not strange when believers hire restaurant servers to break the Sabbath for them? Is it not strange when we hire attendants at gas stations and cashiers at grocery stores to break the Sabbath for the sake of our convenience? Can we in good conscience invite these people to attend church to hear the gospel, when perhaps we have skipped worship in order to hire them to help us travel that day, or when we leave worship early in order to beat the line at the lunch buffet? Can we call them to repentance and to sincere

---

11. See the treatment of Nehemiah 13 in chapter 1.

faith in Jesus Christ while we are in the act of hiring them to break one of the King's laws? If we must keep the sixth commandment in relation to others, then we must keep the fourth commandment in relation to others.

Summary Observations

The pattern the Son of God provided to interpret the commandments of the triune God demands that the Sabbath requires much more than cessation from labor. Too often the fourth commandment has been interpreted in such a manner that it can be kept in perfection with relative ease. Is it not easy to think of the fourth commandment with regard to outward actions only, with little regard to keeping the day holy in heart, speech, and with respect to others? Yet is this not the very problem Jesus confronted when He expounded the sixth commandment in the Sermon on the Mount? Any interpretation of any of the commandments of God that gives the impression that it is *possible* for sinners to keep them is at best suspect. It has become common in Reformed churches to interpret the fourth commandment in a manner out of accord with the way in which all the other commandments are interpreted.

In light of Jesus' principles of interpreting and applying the law of God, we must come to terms with several questions. If you say that the prohibition is "You shall do no work," and that the requirement is "rest," then what kind of "rest" does God require? It cannot be inactivity; therefore, what does it mean to keep the Sabbath holy? If you do not break or keep the Sabbath by thoughts about your employments and recreations, then how else can you apply this commandment to your thoughts? If you cannot break the Sabbath by speaking about labor and recreation, then how is it possible to break it in speech at all? Yet if you do not speak about these things, then what conversation topics do you replace them with? If you do not believe it is a sin to support the labor of others on the Sabbath day, then how does your Sabbath-keeping relate to your neighbor? These are questions with which we must come to terms. Unless other viable answers are supplied from Scripture, there is no better conclusion than this: "The Sabbath is to be sanctified by an holy resting all that day, even from such worldly employments and recreations as are lawful on other days, and spending the whole time in the public and private exercises of God's worship, except so far as is to be taken up in works of necessity and mercy," as well as by avoiding "unnecessary thoughts, words, or works about our worldly employments or recreations" (Westminster Shorter Catechism, Q. 60–61). Can this conclusion be averted without implying that Jesus misinterpreted the sixth commandment? May you reassess how you interpret and live according to the law of God, and may you love the law out of love to your Savior!

CHAPTER EIGHT

Some General Practical Observations

As we apply the principles established so far, we need to consider what Sabbath-keeping should look like in practice. Some people will desire an exhaustive list of activities that are or are not lawful on the Sabbath day. The desire to know how to apply properly the fourth commandment in every circumstance is a legitimate desire, but coming up with an ironclad list of applications is not the method the triune God has given us to apply this or any of His commandments. The law of God applies to every circumstance in life, and it must be applied in innumerable individual instances. Unfortunately, some people have made the minutiae of Sabbath-keeping the litmus test of whether or not a book on the Sabbath is worth reading. Others are thinking right now that everything argued for in this book is already far too detailed, and that the author would have been better off by presenting the broadest principles possible. However, those who desire an exhaustive list of every activity that can be imagined in relation to the Sabbath, as well as those who are concerned with the most basic general principles, will fail to apply the Scriptures properly. The former group desires someone else to do all of their thinking for them, and the latter does not desire to think with care and precision. True biblical ethics, however, always require careful critical thinking on the basis of established biblical principles.

General Remarks

For the sake of clarity, it is important to make a few remarks about the principles that have already been set forth, as well as to add some additional observations that will help to guide you in your Sabbath-keeping. First, everything insisted upon so far consists of *principles* rather than details. These principles have been illustrated and pressed upon your conscience at points, but they are principles nonetheless. Forbidding worldly employments and recreations are principles of Sabbath-keeping necessitated by the purpose and design of the day. The same is true with respect to obedience in thoughts and words, as well as in works. The governing principle that should govern every activity on the Sabbath is that we must call the Sabbath a delight and delight ourselves in the Lord through the means of corporate and private worship. Although many react against a statement such as Shorter Catechism Question 60 regarding how the Sabbath should be sanctified, the genius of such a statement is that it summarizes the biblical principles of Sabbath-keeping without providing a detailed list of applications. In other words, the principles established above provide the necessary criteria for thinking critically in order to apply the fourth commandment in every possible situation. Many are comfortable with only the most general principles of Christian living; yet the question is not which principles make us comfortable, but which principles Scripture requires.

Second, although it is important to focus upon the principles set forth in Scripture, principles necessitate some applications that should be held in common by all. Everyone implicitly recognizes that prohibiting outward acts of murder includes murder committed with a knife, a gun, a club, or any other weapon. Clear examples are useful (and, at times, vitally necessary) in order to understand our principles in tangible forms. This is why I have included obvious examples in this book such as the following: If thoughts about recreations are forbidden on the Sabbath, then thoughts about football are forbidden on the Sabbath. In the Old Testament, God often illustrated the meaning of His laws in a similar manner. God commanded His people to honor His name. When a man cursed God in the midst of a fight, God demonstrated that His commandment should be applied in such cases by ordering the execution of the man. However, even though some applications of a principle are necessary and clear, others are not as clear. To illustrate: Asserting that recreations are inappropriate on the Sabbath is a principle; insisting that children should not play in Little League on the Sabbath is a necessary application of that principle. In contrast, though patronizing the labor of others on the Sabbath is wrong, men's consciences may differ whether or not it is lawful to use public transportation on the Sabbath, provided that it is the only means of attending corporate worship. There is only one legitimate answer to such questions, yet the answers are not always easy to determine, and brethren must exercise charity and patience toward one another in these cases.

This leads to a third important general consideration. We must recognize that not everyone who agrees that the Sabbath should be sanctified for the purposes of worship, excluding worldly employments and recreations, will agree over every application of these principles. One question I have often heard is whether or not it is appropriate to go for a walk with a child in the park on the Lord's Day. Two men sharing the same principles of Sabbath-keeping may legitimately answer this question differently. One man may say that he walks in the park on Sunday afternoons with his son so they can get away from the distractions in the home in order to speak with his son about the things of the Lord, and about his spiritual growth and struggles. Operating upon the same principles, another man avoids the park because in his case the park presents too many distractions, and he believes that he and his son will be hindered from keeping their hearts focused on the purposes of the day. It is important to note that even though these two fathers have arrived at opposite conclusions, both of them are judging what is appropriate on the Sabbath by the same criteria. Disagreements among those who believe that the purpose of the Sabbath day is worship do not always reflect disagreements over principles, as much as the customized struggles and temptations of each individual heart.

Other Practical Observations

In addition to these general observations, there are several others that will help you keep the Sabbath day holy. Following John Owen, I have separated these into duties to be done the evening before the Sabbath and duties to be done on the day itself.

What to Do before the Sabbath

While the night before is not part of the Sabbath itself, it is profitable to use it to prepare for the duties of the next day. The caution that John Owen gave at this point is helpful. Owen argued that preparation for the Sabbath was necessary for two reasons: the glory and majesty of the God with whom we are preparing to spend the day in communion, and the overwhelming tendency for us to be distracted with the activities of the rest of the week.[1] It is next to impossible to rush into the Lord's Day and strive to orient our thoughts, words, and works exclusively to the Lord and His worship by a sudden and almost violent transition. Owen wisely added, however, that we cannot be too insistent as to how others should prepare for Lord's Day worship. Patently, whatever preparation we engage in should actually prepare us for worship. So, for example, mopping floors or doing homework at 11:55 on Saturday evening is probably not the wisest means of preparing for a day in which we are striving not to think about these things (not to mention how tired we will be for worship in the morning). After setting our household affairs in order, Owen recommended meditation, prayer, and family worship.

Although preparing for the Lord's Day is not, strictly speaking, a part of the Lord's Day, it reflects the fact that it takes time and thought for the human mind to shift gears fully from the varied activities of life to a day that, for the most part, excludes them. Preparation for the Lord's Day reminds us that we must lay everything aside for the coming day. If there is still unfinished business on Saturday or business that we know will be pressing on Monday morning, part of our preparation must include entrusting our work

---

1. Owen, *Day of Sacred Rest*, 454–55.

to the Lord, and making sure we are prepared on Saturday for the needs of Monday morning. For example, I became convicted of Sabbath-keeping while I was in college. Professors were not sympathetic to my Sabbath convictions when there was going to be a test on Monday morning. Part of my preparation for the Sabbath meant that I studied as much as I was able to on Saturday. In my preparation for the Lord's Day, I entrusted the exam into God's care, trusting Him for the outcome. Preparation for the Sabbath was, in this case, necessary in order to avoid being distracted on the Lord's Day by the coming exam. Preparing like this is difficult at first, but you will find that you ultimately never lose anything by honoring God's day. Preparing for the Sabbath is not only an implied necessity, but it is also an inestimable help to keep the day with the greatest profit.

What to Do on the Sabbath: One Overarching Principle

A man who desires to marry a young woman often becomes focused on doing whatever is necessary to take her hand in marriage. He works and saves in order to provide for a family. He perseveres through whatever is necessary because the woman he loves and delights in is the clear end and goal of everything he is doing. Similarly, the more you foster a genuine and passionate desire for the worship of God as the goal of your Sabbath-keeping, the more your practical questions will be answered. The more you "call the Sabbath a delight," the fewer questions you will have as to what helps or hinders you from delighting in the Lord of the Sabbath. As you delight in the Lord on the Sabbath, you will also grow in delighting in loving your neighbor on the Sabbath.

Owen argued that the true manner in which we must both guard and exercise our Christian liberty in our Sabbath-keeping is by recognizing that the liberty we have in Christ is exercised by loving submission to His authority. Owen wrote, "Those whose minds are fixed in a spirit of liberty to glorify God in and by this day of rest, seeking after communion with him in the ways of his worship, will be unto themselves a better rule for their words and actions than those who may aim to reckon over all they do or say."[2] Owen reminded his readers that because the Lord Jesus Christ consecrated the first day of the week as the New Testament Sabbath by rising from the dead on that day, loving Christ and worshiping God for His Person and work should be central to our Sabbath-keeping. He added, "Faith truly exercised in bringing the soul into actual subjection unto the authority of Christ in the observance of this day, and directing the thoughts unto a contemplation of the rest that he entered into after his works, with the rest that he hath procured for us to enter into with him, doth more thereby towards the true sanctification of this day than all outward duties can do, performed with a legal spirit, when men are in bondage to the command as taught to them, and dare not do otherwise."[3]

Consider What Facilitates Worship in the Best Manner
Not everyone has the same capacity or ability to engage in spiritual exercises on the Lord's Day. Before my wife and I were married, I spent Sunday afternoons at her parents' home. In her case, it was more profitable to take a nap in the afternoon in order to prepare for evening worship. In my case, it was more profitable to take advantage of the quiet afternoon in order to pray and read edifying literature, or to converse with a friend. In every case of practice on the Sabbath, the same question should be asked: "How can I best keep the principles of the day, and pursue the worship of God in the most profitable and undistracted manner?"

In general, however, sleeping through the Lord's Day should be discouraged. Sleep is not a means of grace. If taking a nap on the Lord's Day is necessary so you can use the means of grace more profitably, then a nap is best. If, however, you need sleep because you stayed up too late the evening before or you are filled with anxiety over the activities of the rest of the week, your own lack

---

2. Owen, *Day of Sacred Rest*, 447. See also McGraw, "Five Reasons Why the Sabbath Was Designed for Worship."

3. Owen, *Day of Sacred Rest*, 449–50.

of preparation has hindered your ability to the means of grace and you should repent. Jonathan Edwards exhorted, "Improve your Sabbaths, and especially the time of public worship, which is the most precious part. Lose it not, either in sleep, or in carelessness, inattention, and wandering imaginations. How sottish are they who waste away, not only their common, but holy time, yea the very season of attendance on the holy ordinances of God."[4] The primary benefit of the Sabbath day comes through the means of grace, and you should structure the day so you are able to spend as much of it using the means of grace as you are able.

Give Preference to Corporate Worship above Private

The Sabbath should be occupied with the public and private exercises of the worship of God, but corporate worship should be regarded as more glorious than private. At the present day, most of the counsel directed toward godly Christian living addresses only private practices of devotion. The importance of corporate worship has largely been lost. How many of the psalms, such as Psalm 84, record the grief of the psalmist because he was not able to go with the multitude to the house of God? David longed to appear before God in corporate worship as the deer pants for the brooks of water (Ps. 42:1). It is in corporate worship that "God is in you of a truth" (1 Cor. 14:25). As we gather together as a church in the name of the Lord Jesus Christ, He is there in our midst (Matt. 18:20).

Most of the duties set forth in connection with the Sabbath in Scripture relate to corporate rather than private worship. The "song for the Sabbath day" included morning and evening worship (Ps. 92:1–4). If the church of which you are a member has evening as well as morning worship, if you are at all able, attend both services. We often undervalue what happens in corporate worship simply because we lack the faith to believe that God is there in our midst. Although some of us gather together in small congregations

---

4. Cited in John Carrick, *The Preaching of Jonathan Edwards* (Edinburgh: Banner of Truth, 2008), 176.

in simple buildings with poor singing, we must come to corporate worship recognizing that, in a peculiar manner, we enter into the heavenly sanctuary and join the chorus of an innumerable company of angels. A large part of keeping the Sabbath is taking advantage of corporate worship. This is the high point of the day, and it is the part of the Sabbath that most closely resembles heaven.[5]

One Remaining Factor

One last aspect that should be taken into account is that the guilt of doing what is inherently sinful is doubled when it is committed on the Sabbath day. As Edwards wrote, "How provoking it must be to God, when men do those things on that day—which he has sanctified and set apart to be spent in the immediate exercises of religion—which are not fit to be done on common days, which are impure and wicked whenever they are done!"[6] God did not give the Sabbath to be a burden to man; He gave it to him out of love. To live worldly lives on the Sabbath not only spurns the authority of God, but it also spurns His love in giving us such a blessed day for our own good. Thomas Shepard noted, "The same sins which are committed upon other days of the week are then provoking sins; but to

---

5. Although he urged the church not to neglect private worship, Baxter made an interesting observation on this point: "My judgment is, that in those places where the public worship taketh up almost the whole day, it is no sin to attend upon it to the utmost, as to omit all family and secret exercises, *as cannot be done without omission of the public.* And that where the public exercises allow but little time at home, the family duty should take up all that little time, except what some shorter, secret prayers or meditations may have, which will not hinder family duties.... The Lord's Day is principally set apart for public worship, and the more private or secret is as it were included in the public.... It is turning God's worship into ceremony and superstition, to think that you must necessarily put up the same prayers in a closet, which you have put up in the family or church, when you have not time for both." Richard Baxter, *The Divine Appointment of the Lord's Day,* in *The Practical Works of Richard Baxter* (London, 1846; repr. Morgan, Pa.: Soli Deo Gloria, 2000), 3:901 (emphasis added).

6. Jonathan Edwards, "The Perpetuity and Change of the Sabbath," in *Works,* 2:102.

commit these sins on the Sabbath is to double the evil of them."[7] Keeping the Sabbath ought to set your mind upon faith in Christ and obedience to your Father in heaven more than on other days, since you have greater means to help you on the Sabbath than on other days. If you fall into notorious sins on the Sabbath, they are more worthy of blame than on other days because you were given more means to prevent them. Neglecting these means despises the grace and glory of God. As Shepard asked, "Is the infinite majesty and glory of God so vile in your eyes that you do not think him worthy of special attendance one day in a week?"[8]

None of this is meant to discourage you in your pursuit of holiness. If you do not continually see the difficulties of holiness, and you are not uncovering more and more of the sin of your heart, you are not pursuing the Christian life in earnest. The Christian life can be lived only by the power of the Holy Spirit working what would otherwise be impossible in the hearts and lives of sinful people. Christians must never be afraid to be convicted of sin. There is no condemnation of those who are in Christ Jesus (Rom. 8:1). The righteous requirements of the law have been fulfilled in us through Him who came in the likeness of sinful flesh to condemn sin in His flesh (Rom. 8:3–4). The knowledge of any previously undiscovered sin should grieve the hearts of believers; but believers are brought to grief over sin by sinning against the love of a kind and tenderhearted Father, a gentle Savior, and a sanctifying Spirit. The conviction of sin is always painful for a child of God, but it should always be welcome. How else will we be conformed to the image and likeness of Christ? How else will we reflect the glory of God more and more, and enjoy greater blessings of fellowship and communion with Him?

---

7. Shepard, *Theses Sabbaticae*, 267.
8. Shepard, *Theses Sabbaticae*, 268.

Conclusions

There was a certain inevitability about the pattern of Sabbath-keeping proposed by the Westminster divines. In fact, as Richard Gaffin has noted, most have not taken into account the degree to which the Westminster doctrine of the Sabbath is an integral part of the entire system of theology contained in those documents.[9] The place of the fourth commandment within the first table of the law demands that any proper view of keeping the Sabbath should primarily have respect to God and His worship, just as the first three commandments do. The pastors at Westminster could not conclude anything less than that the ultimate purpose of the day was worship rather than rest. This automatically meant that all worldly employments and recreations that were lawful on other days should be ruled out on the Sabbath day. Since every command of God reaches beyond the outward actions and touches the speech and thoughts of men, how could they have concluded otherwise than they did concerning our speech and the state of our hearts and minds on the Sabbath day? If what is not lawful for ourselves is not lawful for others, and we must love our neighbors as ourselves, how could the divines believe that God permits His servants to support others in their Sabbath-breaking? It is important to grasp that it is inconsistent to abandon the Westminster doctrine of the Sabbath without also abandoning the biblical and Reformed position regarding the proper interpretation of the law of God. Men do not always work out their positions consistently, yet rejecting the position that the Sabbath is a day of worship excluding worldly recreation and labor, and that must be kept in heart and speech, threatens to take apart at the seams the entire Westminster doctrine of the law of God. This illustrates a radical theological shift that cannot be made consistently without entirely reevaluating the law itself.

---

9. Richard Gaffin, "Westminster and the Sabbath," in *The Westminster Confession into the 21st Century* (Geanies House, U.K.: Christian Focus Publications, 2003), 1:126–28.

In addition to being out of accord with the Reformed position on the law of God, there are severe theological and practical consequences to assuming that the Sabbath requires rest from labor only. Have you considered that this assumption tacitly asserts that people may keep the Sabbath in perfection, and that very easily? As long as we do not go to work that day and attend corporate worship, we have done all that is required of us by God on the Lord's Day. Which of the commandments is this "easy" for sinners to keep? The fourth commandment represents 10 percent of the summary of God's moral law. Are you willing to say that you can keep 10 percent of God's law in absolute perfection? Are we, as sinners, *entirely* dependent upon the blood and righteousness of Christ, or do we need His redemption for breaking 90 percent of His law only? Is the Sabbath the one commandment among the first four that is not concerned primarily with the worship of God? Is the fourth commandment the only commandment that cannot be broken in heart and speech, as well as in outward behavior? In other words, if you do not see the utter impossibility of keeping the fourth commandment, then there is something wrong with how you view this commandment. This is either a glaring inconsistency respecting the application of God's law, or it reflects the fact that many believers have allowed the meaning and proper uses of the law of God to slip though their fingers.

If you do not believe that you fall into this error in theory, you may still be guilty of it in practice. If someone cautions you about speaking too much about your job on Sunday, how do you respond to them? Do you object that they are going beyond the bounds of God's law? Does the fourth commandment have any practical relevance in your life beyond your outward actions? In theory, you may not believe that you may keep any of God's laws in absolute perfection. You may acknowledge that you are in need of the cleansing blood of Christ for every thought and action and that you can do nothing without Him. But do you have room in your theology ever to be convicted of Sabbath-breaking? Should you not rather have abundant material for confessing your sins against the Sabbath every week? It is a bad sign if you have no practical conviction of sin with respect to the Sabbath and have no conscious dependence upon the Spirit of Christ in striving to keep it. This is a sure indicator that there is something wrong with your practical conception of the fourth commandment. This may be true even if you ardently defend the Westminster position on Sabbath-keeping. It is not those who speak most vehemently about keeping the Sabbath who love the Sabbath, but those who see the blessedness of the Sabbath and cast themselves in dependence on their God for His help to keep it holy. To apply this commandment to our lives, we must first see the scope of the commandment and our inability to keep it. Then we must return to the commandment cleansed of our sins through the blood of Christ, compelled by His love to serve Him. Only then will we call the Sabbath a delight and rejoice that God has set apart an entire day for the purposes of grateful and heartfelt worship.

CHAPTER NINE

Legalism?

John Newton wrote, "Ignorance of the nature and design of the law is at the bottom of most religious mistakes."[1] Why should a chapter on legalism, which addresses the fundamental relationship between the law and the gospel, follow rather than precede a chapter on how to interpret the law properly? The reason I have taken this approach is that most disagreements between believers begin with some point of Christian practice. It is only after different positions collide in a practical setting that we begin asking what underlying questions have caused the conflict in the first place. In biblical counseling, Jay Adams has observed that resolving a conflict between two parties begins by addressing the problem immediately presented. After evaluating the initial information, the counselor begins to peel back layers until he discovers the underlying issues at the heart of the conflict. It is only at that point he can begin to counsel effectively and to resolve the conflict.[2] One complaint commonly brought against people who hold to a "strict" or "Puritan" view of Sabbath-keeping is that this interpretation of God's law demonstrates that they are guilty of legalism. This accusation often reflects a misunderstanding of what "legalism" is and, more fundamentally, the proper relationship between the law and the gospel in Scripture. For this reason, I will provide an overview of the role of the law of God throughout

---

1. Cited in Plumer, *Law of God*, 9.
2. Jay Adams, *Competent to Counsel: Introduction to Nouthetic Counseling* (Grand Rapids: Zondervan, 1970), 148–51.

redemptive history, demonstrate what legalism is not, examine what legalism is, establish the true problem behind this accusation, and make application to Sabbath-keeping.

The Law of God in Redemptive History

There is no place in the history of biblical revelation in which the law does not hold a predominant place and play an essential part. There are three fundamental settings in which the law of God is found in Scripture. First, the law of God was written upon Adam's heart in the garden of Eden. This is implied by Paul's statement in Romans 2:14–15 concerning the unbelieving Gentiles, who did not have access to the Scriptures: "For when the Gentiles, which have not the law, do by nature the things contained in the law, these, having not the law, are a law unto themselves: which shew the work of the law written in their hearts." If it is true that fallen people retain some remnants of the work of God's law written upon their hearts, then how much more would Adam and Eve have had the same law written upon their hearts before becoming sinners? The law of God upon the heart of man is part of what it means for man to be the image and likeness of God. This is the only basis upon which Paul could make this statement.

The difference between the law written on the heart of man prior to the Fall and subsequent to the Fall, however, is the difference between the reflection provided by a perfectly intact mirror and a shattered mirror. After the Fall, the law remained upon the heart of man as a reflection of God's own holy character, but man did not like to retain God in his knowledge, suppressed the truth in unrighteousness, and has done everything in his power not to reflect the glory of his Creator (Rom. 1:28; 8:7). On the one hand, this means that man can never successfully eradicate the knowledge of his Creator through his sinful rebellion. On the other hand, it means that man can no longer have any certain and clear knowledge of the law of God without revelation and instruction from God.

For this reason, in the course of time God republished that same law on two tablets of stone and delivered them to Moses. This is the second setting in which the law appeared. The law written upon the heart of man was defaced by sin. The tablets that God gave to Moses summarized the law that had been suppressed and obscured by sin and made it clear once again by putting it into writing. This is partially why the apostle Paul argued that the purpose of the law as written was to leave men without excuse before God (Rom. 3:19–20). The law written upon Adam's heart in the garden of Eden was like a book that had gone out of print. The republication of the law on tablets of stone was the reprinting of the same book in a second edition. By the time of the reprinting, however, the audience had changed and no longer enjoyed reading the book. To put it another way, in the garden prior to the Fall, the law of God was engraved upon Adam's heart, and keeping the law was "instinctive." On Mount Sinai, the law of God was engraved upon tablets of stone; it was now repulsive to fallen human nature. In addition to imparting knowledge of the perfection and glorious character of God, as well as providing a complete guide for a life that was pleasing to God, the law now brought the knowledge of sin and the wrath of God in response to sin (Rom. 3:20; 7:7).[3]

---

3. For these reasons many Reformed authors have treated the covenant made between God and Israel at Mount Sinai as a republication of the covenant of works. This was certainly Owen's position, as he sets it forth clearly in section 4 of his *Day of Sacred Rest*. In his notes to *The Marrow of Modern Divinity*, Thomas Boston noted that in addition to the author of that book (Edward Fisher), many notable divines adopted this position, including men such as George Gillespie. Boston himself argued that the preface to the Ten Commandments, along with several comparable statements in the Pentateuch, made it abundantly clear that the primary character of the Mosaic economy was that of the covenant of grace, which would come to its full fruition in Jesus Christ. However, due to his exegesis of Romans 2 and 3 and Galatians 3 and 4 (which was the same reasoning provided by Owen), Boston also asserted the presence of the covenant of works, functioning in a manner subservient to the covenant of grace. Its sole purpose was to drive men to the knowledge of their sin into the arms of Christ alone. See Edward Fisher, *The Marrow of Modern Divinity*, in *The Complete Works of Thomas Boston* (1853; repr., Stoke-on-Trent, U.K.: Tentmaker Publications, 2002), 7:194–202. For an

The third setting in which the law appears is in the new covenant, which was ratified through the blood of Christ (Matt. 26; Heb. 9:14–16). Part of the provisions of the new covenant was to take the *same law* that was written upon Adam's heart and republished at Sinai (as a source of condemnation to sinners ever since) and to write it upon the tablets of men's hearts (Jer. 31; Ezek. 36). Christ did not only deliver men from the guilt of their sins and impute His own righteousness to them, but by the work of His Spirit, He is writing the law of God upon the tablets of their hearts. The Spirit is writing the same law, which was obscured through Adam's Fall, upon redeemed hearts. The almighty hand that wrote the law upon tablets of stone is once again writing it upon the tablets of men's hearts. In this case, however, the transcription is gradual rather than instantaneous. Christ will complete His inscription when those who believe in Him enter into His presence at death and are perfected at the resurrection. All of this is to say that in His elect, the Lord Jesus Christ is reversing the effects of the Fall from the inside out. This reversal begins by restoring the manner in which man relates to the law. In theological terminology, this is the essence of sanctification. Man fell by sinning against God's law, bringing corruption to himself and to the entire created order. Christ is the end of the law for righteousness to all who believe (Rom. 10:4), and He is gradually renewing the entire created order by redeeming and sanctifying sinners and by putting all His enemies under His feet (Rom. 8; Col. 1; 1 Cor. 15). There is, therefore, no stage in the history of redemption and God's purposes for the world, whether before or after the Fall, in the Old Testament or in the New Testament, in which the law of God does not hold the utmost importance.[4]

---

alternate view see John Flavel, *A Reply to Mr. Cary's Solemn Call*, in *The Works of John Flavel* (1820; repr., Edinburgh: Banner of Truth, 1997), 6:324–25.

4. See Herman Bavinck, *Reformed Dogmatics: Holy Spirit, Church, and New Creation*, trans. John Vriend, ed. John Bolt (Grand Rapids: Baker, 2008), 4:455; and Fisher, *Marrow of Modern Divinity*, 173, 198. John Murray has also written an insightful article on the place of the law in biblical revelation. John Murray, "The Sanctity of the Moral Law," in *Collected Writings*, 1:193–204.

What Legalism Is Not

It is in this context and with these facts in view that we must examine the charge of "legalism." Legalism is not a term that appears in Scripture, but it is a term often utilized in discussions about Scripture and must therefore be evaluated in light of Scripture. A seminary student initially learns in his study of the biblical languages that the words used most frequently in the ancient world are the words that have the broadest and most elastic range of meaning. The same is true in the realm of theological language. The term "legalism" is used so widely on a popular level in the church today that it often possesses as many meanings as people who use the term. On a popular level, the term "legalism" often refers to justification by works, to requiring what is beyond the law of God, to keeping the law of God too strictly, to having any use for law at all, to quoting from the Old Testament, and so forth. Every use of the term "legalism," however, refers in some measure to the keeping of law, and it always has a decidedly negative if not derogatory connotation (who refers to himself as a "legalist"?). In the broadest general terms, therefore, "legalism" may be defined as an improper use of law. The charge of "legalism" against Sabbath-keeping is a serious one. Thus it is important to establish what does not and what does constitute an improper use of the law of God.

Legalism Cannot Refer to Keeping the Law

The fact that legalism cannot legitimately be used to refer to the continuing relevance of the law of God as a guide to godly living should already be clear from the discussion above regarding the role of the law in redemptive history. Those who take this position, if they have any use for the law of God, generally relegate its use to man in his pre-converted condition. People who assert that believers should not be concerned about keeping the law of God as a rule of life in any sense will ordinarily level the charge of legalism at the bare mention of law, especially when it is law taken from the Old Testament. In the New Testament, however, sin is defined by behavior that is against the law: "Whosoever committeth sin transgresseth also the law: for sin is the transgression of the law" (1 John 3:4). The word for "law" in the Greek language is *nomos*. When the Greeks wanted to negate an idea, they simply added an "a" to the beginning of a word. For example, an *atheist* is someone who is against theism or the belief in God. In a similar manner, when the apostle John provided this definition for sin, he did so by using the Greek term for law (*nomos*) with the prefix "a." If an atheist by definition is against theism, then according to John sin by definition is against law (Greek: *he harmaria estiv he anomia*). The law of God is the measuring rod by which mankind knows both sin and duty. For this reason, the apostle Paul wrote, "I had not known sin, but by the law" (Rom. 7:7).

In other words, without the law of God, the very concept of sin is meaningless. For this reason, the Westminster Shorter Catechism has provided a concise and accurate definition of the biblical idea of sin: "Sin is any want of conformity unto, or transgression of the Law of God" (Question 14). If the law of God has no relevance to the Christian, how could he ever pray the Lord's Prayer, which teaches him to pray for the forgiveness of sin? If any man is so bold or foolish as to say that he has no sin, John asserts that such a man is self-deceived and that the truth is not in him (1 John 1:8). As believers, our hope before God is that when we confess our sins, God is faithful and just to forgive us our sins and cleanse us from all unrighteousness (v. 9). If you take away the continuing relevance of the law for those who have been redeemed by Christ, who is the end of the law for righteousness (Rom. 10:4), with it you take away the possibility of identifying and confessing sin. Sin is defined only by the law of God; believers must be able to identify and confess sin; therefore, the law of God continues to be relevant to believers. If you must confess sin, then you must avoid sin as well. If you must avoid sin, then you must know the rule that defines sin. If you are a believer, you cannot avoid the law without becoming indifferent to sin.

These truths necessarily imply that the law of God must have further relevance to the Christian than merely the negative use of being convicted of sin. A Christian by definition cannot continually commit sin or live a life in which sin reigns unchecked and unmolested (1 John 3:9). Believers have died to the power of sin through the death of Christ, and they have been raised to walk in newness of life through the resurrection of Christ. For these reasons, believers must not present their members as slaves to sin to obey sin; but since sin no longer has dominion over them, they must present their members to God as slaves of righteousness (Rom. 6). If sin is law-breaking, then obedience is law-keeping. Obedience to Christ does not entail keeping the law as a covenant of works in order to justify ourselves in the sight of God. Obedience to Christ is keeping the law of God out of gratitude in a spirit of worship and thanksgiving as a response to the covenant of grace. The Lord Jesus Christ took the danger out of the law on behalf of the believer by keeping the law of God on our behalf and by offering Himself as a sacrifice to satisfy divine justice.

It is obviously the law of God, which is summarized in the Ten Commandments, that is in view in these passages. There is no other law that can properly convict men and bind them to their duty. If believers must be concerned about sin, then they must be concerned about the law. If believers must be concerned about keeping themselves from sin, then they must be concerned with identifying sin and duty through the use of law. If a Christian becomes a legalist de facto by concerning himself with the law of God, then a Christian also becomes a legalist by loving Christ through keeping Christ's commandments (John 15:14). It is not an abuse of the law of God when Christians look to it as the standard for holiness and personal godliness. What other standard can possibly substitute or replace the law of God as a rule of righteous living, since it is a perfect transcript of the character of the triune God? So far from being unconcerned about personal godliness or righteousness as defined by the law of God, the Lord Jesus Christ asserted, "Except your righteousness shall exceed the righteousness of the scribes and Pharisees, ye shall in no case enter into the kingdom of heaven" (Matt. 5:20). Jesus' intent in this passage is not to set forth the qualifications for the justification of sinners, but to present a factual *description* of justified sinners who are entering His kingdom.

Legalism Cannot Refer to the Careful and
Particular Keeping of God's Law

If "legalism" refers to an improper use of the law of God, then it is also wrong to use the term to describe a careful attention to the law in all of its particular details and applications. In modern society, we often use the term "strict" as a derogatory term. When we say that parents are being strict with their children, we usually mean that those parents are being harsh toward their children. However, it is a mistake to assume that adhering to a particular standard is harsh or burdensome simply because it is all-encompassing. If we must be concerned with the law of God at all, we must be concerned with the whole law of God. There is not one law of God that requires perfect, personal, and perpetual obedience in order to drive men to Christ and another law of God that requires imperfect, general, and occasional obedience as a rule of life. Although no mere man since the Fall is able to keep the law of God perfectly, there is still no other standard of obedience, duty, and above all, love for the Christian. Your standard of godliness must reflect the God into whose image you are being conformed. For this reason, Jonathan Edwards wrote, "The strictness of God's law is a principle cause of man's enmity against him."[5] It is thus illegitimate to reject a view of the Sabbath that sets up a standard that no fallen man, even if he is redeemed, is able to keep perfectly. The manner in which we must pursue obedience to the law of God under the grace of the gospel will be dealt with in more detail below, but for the time being we must give careful heed to the warning of William Plumer: "The human heart earnestly pleads for lawlessness. Men are much accustomed to yield to public opinion around them. The fear of being esteemed singular is a snare to thousands. He who is not prepared to stand in a minority of one with a majority of millions against him, will not keep a good conscience respecting the Lord's Day."[6]

---

5. Edwards, "Men Naturally God's Enemies,"133.
6. Plumer, *Law of God*, 324.

What Legalism Is

It is equally important to consider what legalism legitimately refers to. What constitutes an abuse or improper use of the law of God? Does keeping the entire Sabbath as a day of worship in thought, word, and deed fall legitimately under the category of legalism? "Legalism" is a term that may appropriately describe at least three errors addressed in Scripture: justification by the works of the law, adding to or taking away from the law of God, and sanctification by the works of the law.

Justification by the Works of the Law

Justification by the works of the law is the most flagrant and most deadly form of legalism. This is legalism in the most proper sense of the term. Justification by the works of the law can be entire or partial. In either case, this form of legalism is like a deadly poison that spreads rapidly through the spiritual veins: inevitably, the blood flows to the heart and the poison kills the man. Although often mentioned, pure forms of justification by the works of the law are actually quite rare. It is only the most deluded people who have ever believed they are able to achieve the perfect righteousness demanded by the law of God for their justification. Even those who have believed in the hypothetical possibility of choosing a life devoid of sin have found it difficult to deny the plain fact that there is no man who has not actually committed sin in his life.[7] Writing to those who had already come to the Lord Jesus Christ for salvation, the apostle John wrote, "If we say we have no sin, we deceive ourselves, and the truth is not in us" (1 John 1:8). Not only is the person

---

7. D. M. Lloyd-Jones has noted an example of this in the experience of John Wesley, who adhered to a mild form of Christian perfectionism. Even a Pelagian such as Charles Finney did not deny that all men in this world have committed sin prior to conversion. *The Puritans: Their Origins and Successors* (Edinburgh: Banner of Truth, 1987), 304–14. R. C. Sproul has noted that even Pelagius believed that all men have actually sinned by following the bad example set by Adam and others. R. C. Sproul, *Willing to Believe: The Controversy over Free Will* (Grand Rapids: Baker, 1997), 33–45.

who says that he has no sin self-deceived, but John added that this person implicitly makes God (who has testified that all men have sin) to be a liar (v. 10). The perfection required by the law of God is absolute. He who desires to be justified by his own good works "is a debtor to do the whole law" (Gal. 5:3). This is why the apostle Paul confidently asserted: "By the deeds of the law there shall no flesh shall be justified in his sight: for by the law is the knowledge of sin" (Rom. 3:20). Most people have enough modesty to acknowledge they are not perfect; yet if they are not perfect, they cannot be accepted in the sight of God through their own works. Therefore, Paul warned soberly: "You have become estranged from Christ, you who attempt to be justified by the law; you have fallen from grace" (Gal. 5:4, my translation).

In the realm of justification, the grace of God through faith in Christ and the works of the law are mutually exclusive categories. Paul wrote, "And if by grace, then it is no more of works; otherwise grace is no more grace. But if it be of works, then it is no more grace; otherwise work is no more work" (Rom. 11:6). Although most people know they cannot achieve the perfect righteousness demanded by the holy law of God, multitudes believe they will be saved in part by grace and in part by obedience. These people act as though God will forgive them by His grace for those areas in which they fail, but that they can take it from there the rest of the time. This appears to be the "default" position among the human race, yet this is just as far from the gospel and the kingdom of God as is the position that man can perfectly fulfill the terms of God's perfect law. What if you believe you can do some good things that are pleasing to God, even though you need forgiveness for many things? If it is of works, then it is no longer of grace; and if it is of grace, then it is no longer of works. What if you plead that you should be accepted because you have been a good husband and father, or a self-sacrificing mother? If it is of works, then it is no longer of grace; and if it is of grace, then it is no longer of works. What if you have regretted the sins you have committed against others, and even asked for their forgiveness with great personal difficultly? Should not God accept you now? If it is of works, then it is no longer of grace; if it is of grace, then it is no longer of works.

The fact is that there is not a single "good" act you have ever committed that you have done wholeheartedly out of love to God and for His glory in every respect. The greatest sins in the eyes of God are not ordinarily the greatest sins in the eyes of men. If you have not loved the Lord your God above all things, in all things, and through all things, then all of your so-called righteous deeds are nothing but filthy rags in His sight (Isa. 64:6). Your good works not only do not impress God, but they are repulsive to Him. If a king commands his subjects to go to war, and they go to war on behalf of his enemies, have they obeyed the king's commands? In the same manner, if you do what is outwardly good, but have not done so for the sake of the King of Glory, then you have made yourself His enemy by your "good works." Who can justify himself by the works of the law? If Adam failed in innocence, then sinners cannot even begin to put their hands to the plow. The partial dependence on our own works, which is implicitly promoted in Roman Catholicism and in many non-Christian religions, is as far from the gospel of Jesus Christ as the most deluded perfectionist who has ever lived. If this is your position today, then you are as far from the gospel of Jesus Christ as you can possibly be.[8]

---

8. In the *Marrow of Modern Divinity*, the legalist (Nomista) presents his own spiritual condition to his pastor (Evangelista). In this description, the legalist goes through three stages of thought. He first describes himself as trying to keep the law in its external form only. After learning that the law requires perfection in the inner man as well as in the outward man, the legalist tried to keep the law in its perfection. After despairing of his ability to observe God's righteous standard perfectly, the legalist did the best he thought he could to keep the law and then trusted in Christ only at the points at which he believed he failed. This was the first time in his description of his experience that he even mentioned Christ. After hearing his case, the pastor responded, "Why, truly, I must tell you, it appears to me by this relation, that you have gone as far in the way of the covenant of works as the apostle Paul did before his conversion; but yet, for aught I see, you have not gone in the right

This first form of legalism is the polar opposite of the gospel. Hear the glorious terms of the gospel: "But after that the kindness and the love of God our Savior toward man appeared, *not by works of righteousness which we have done, but according to his mercy he saved us,* by the washing of regeneration and renewing of the Holy Ghost, which he shed out on us abundantly through Jesus Christ our Savior, that being *justified by his grace* we should be made heirs according the hope of eternal life" (Titus 3:4–7, emphasis added). "Where is boasting then? It is excluded. By what law? Of works? Nay: but by the law of faith. Therefore we conclude that *a man is justified by faith without the deeds of the law*" (Rom. 3:27–28, emphasis added). "For by grace are ye saved through faith; and that not of yourselves; it is the gift of God, *not of works,* lest any man should boast" (Eph. 2:8–9, emphasis added). "But what things were gain to me, those I counted loss for Christ. Yea doubtless and I count all things as loss for the excellency of the knowledge of Christ Jesus my Lord: for whom I have suffered the loss of all things, and do count them but dung that I may win [gain] Christ and be found in him, *not having mine own righteousness, which is of the law, but that which is through the faith of Christ,* the righteousness which is of God by faith" (Phil. 3:7–9, emphasis added). Where do you stand in relation to the Lord Jesus Christ? You must be forgiven *for all,* or you will not be forgiven *at all.* Justification must be all of Christ, or it will be none of Christ. If you hope to be accepted by God by your own good works, either in whole or in part, or by any means that does not depend wholly and only upon Jesus Christ through faith in Him, then you have been engulfed by a form of legalism that excludes you from the kingdom of God as long as you remain under it. In this state, you will never know why the love of Christ passes knowledge (Eph. 3). The doctrine of Sabbath-keeping as it is set forth in the Westminster Standards by no means falls into this form of legalism, since this form of legalism is as thoroughly opposed to the gospel as night is to day.

---

way to the truth of the gospel; and therefore I question whether you be as yet truly come to Christ." Fisher, *Marrow of Modern Divinity,* 230.

Adding to or Taking Away from the Law of God

The next form of legalism is not relegated to those who are excluded from the kingdom of God, but it may be common among those who are within the kingdom of God. In the case of Christians who are guilty of this form of legalism, their faith is built upon the foundation of the grace of God in Christ. The abuse of the law in their case has occurred at the point where they have set up an ethical standard for godly living that is not *identical* to the law of God in every respect. It will be immediately obvious to most that adding to the commands of the law is a form of legalism, but it may seem less obvious that taking away from the law is equally a form of legalism. Yet in every place in which we are warned not to add to the law, we are equally warned against subtracting from the law.

Adding to the law of God is legalism, or an abuse of the law of God. In Deuteronomy 4:2, the Lord said, "Ye shall not add unto the word which I command you, neither shall ye diminish ought from it, that ye may keep the commandments of the Lord your God which I command you." In Deuteronomy 12:32, the Lord reiterated the same instructions, with particular regard to corporate worship: "What thing soever I command you, observe to do it; thou shalt not add thereto, or diminish from it." When we add to the law of God, we are implicitly charging the law with imperfection. In fact, when we add to the law we are implicitly charging God with imperfection, since it is His glorious being and character the law was designed to reflect. This is a grave error. For example, since Jesus' first miracle was turning water into wine at a wedding, when we declare it a sin to drink wine at all we are implying that the law of God, which Jesus never violated, is an imperfect or insufficient rule of life. Likewise, the Pharisees demonstrated the monstrously shameful effects of this form of legalism when they sought to accuse Jesus of sin for healing a man on the Sabbath day (John 5:16). In both of these cases, practices are imposed by men upon others, which are neither commanded nor necessarily inferred from the principles set forth in the Ten Commandments. If God's law is a perfectly consistent and comprehensive rule of life, then any practices man adds to the law of God are inevitably in opposition to the law of God.

The error of taking away from the law of God is not, as it may at first appear, the opposite error of adding to the law of God. When we take away from the law of God, we invariably do so for one of two reasons: either we have not understood the law of God at some point, or we seek to replace the law of God with a standard that is less intimidating and less stringent in its requirements. When we take away from the law of God, we end up setting aside the commandments of God and replacing them with the traditions of men (Matt. 15:8–9). God rebuked the Israelites through Isaiah saying, "Forasmuch as this people draw near with their mouth, and with their lips do honor me, but have removed their heart far from me, and their fear toward me is taught by the precept of men" (Isa. 29:13). Most of the conflict between Jesus and the Pharisees revolved around this point, and Jesus responded to this error in a large portion of the Sermon on the Mount. Everyone has a code of ethics he must apply to every situation in life. When men do not apply the law of God as their standard in any given situation, they will inevitably apply some other standard. If you take away from the law of God, you will always add to the law of God.

This is the true reason why taking away from the law of God is a form of legalism. Adding to the law of God and taking away from the law of God both implicitly attack the sovereignty and infinite wisdom of God as the only lawgiver. There is a wonderfully balanced statement regarding this matter in the Westminster Confession of Faith: "God alone is Lord of the conscience, and hath left it free from the doctrines and commandments of men, which are, in any thing, contrary to his word, or beside it, in matters of faith and worship" (WCF 20.2). If keeping the Sabbath as a sacred day of worship, to the exclusion of both worldly employments and recreations, is adding to the law of God, then indeed it is a form of legalism. However, if these principles of Sabbath-keeping are the necessary implications of keeping the day holy, then those who do not love the Sabbath and delight in God's holy day in this manner, whether intentionally or unintentionally, have become guilty of a subtle form of legalism. The biblical standard for godliness must be *identical* with the perpetually binding moral law of God. The primary question, therefore, is not whether we must be concerned with man's law, but whether we are concerned with God's law or with a law of our own making.

Sanctification by the Works of the Law

This last category of legalism is the subtlest of all, and it is perhaps one of the greatest causes of spiritual trouble and difficulty for God's people. Only God's people can commit this form of legalism. Sin is an ever-present reality in the lives of believers. The presence of sin is a painful reality for Christians, but they must come to terms with the fact that they will never obey God in perfection in any particular instance in this life. The presence of sin did not hinder God from freely bestowing His grace upon His people when they first believed, and it does not keep them from His grace as they strive to imitate Him as dearly beloved children (Eph. 5:1). It is a great mistake to say in an unqualified manner that justification is by grace and that sanctification is by the works of the law. It is true, however, that the law is the only possible standard for sanctification. Christ is the pattern of sanctification, and the law is a transcript of the pattern He set. Though it is true that the law is the lamp that lights the pathway of Christians (Ps. 119:105), believers must pursue sanctification and obedience to the law by faith in Christ, as much as they do in their justification. We have an incessant tendency for self-reliance and independence. However, we can never overestimate the dependence we must have on the Holy Spirit for our sanctification, through faith in the promises of God. Christians may believe in the doctrine of justification by faith alone in Christ alone. They may believe they are utterly helpless and unable to do any good thing apart from the grace of God. Yet the same Christians may conduct themselves in their relationship with God as though this relationship depends entirely upon their obedience to the law, rather than upon the obedience of the Lord Jesus Christ.

The error of legalism in sanctification acts as a two-edged sword. On the one hand, we strive to grow in holiness by our own strength without utter dependence upon the power of the Holy Spirit and the promises of God. On the other hand, when we rediscover the fact that in our flesh no good thing dwells (Rom. 7:18), we plunge into despair and act as though we cannot bear to bring ourselves into the presence of God due to the depths of our failures. This tends to lead to a downward spiral. We begin to think that we are unworthy of Christ because of our sins. This is true of course, but we begin to act upon the feeling that we cannot come to Him because of our continual failures. Perhaps we ask ourselves, "How can saving grace dwell in my heart when I have so much sin remaining in me? How can I struggle with sin so greatly if I have died to the power of sin so that it should not have dominion over me? Have not many others *outwardly* appeared to be much more godly than myself, such as Judas Iscariot, who were children of Satan rather than children of God?" The problem with this line of thought is that it is inevitably self-defeating. If the presence of sin in your life is the cause of doubting the grace of God in your life, how are you likely to respond? You will think that if only you are able to get rid of this one sin, your problems will be solved! You begin to question your warrant to come to the throne of grace to find help in your time of need, so you do not seek the grace of God by faith to enable you to overcome your sin. The believer must trust in the grace of the Lord Jesus Christ by believing in His promises for sanctification as much as for justification. He has become for us wisdom from God and righteousness, *sanctification*, and redemption (1 Cor. 1:30). If you try to "repent" without faith in Christ, are you not *acting* like the man who says he trusts in Christ to forgive him of his past failures, yet tries to stand on his own from then on? Your creed may be, "Through faith alone, in Christ alone, and by the grace of God alone," but your life and practice give the lie to your creed. Taking the eyes of your faith off of Christ is the likely cause of your troubles in the first place. When the first conviction of sin sets in, you must take your sin immediately to Christ. You must plead your weakness and inability before

Him. You must plead His blood to cleanse you. You must plead His promises to the effect that you have died to the power of sin and that sin will no longer have dominion over you! You must ask Him to grant you repentance and to work in you to will and to do of His good pleasure according to His promises. You must plead with Him the fact that you have been created in Christ Jesus for good works, and you must act only upon these principles. This process alone will enable you to grow in holiness and to avoid conceiving of your relationship with God in a legalistic manner, instead of from faith to faith (Rom. 1:18), from beginning to end. Christ is the first and the last, the beginning and the end, the Alpha and the Omega; He is so as your Creator, and He must be so in every aspect of your salvation.

It should be obvious by now that this does not imply that dependence upon the grace of God in Christ for sanctification means you must sit quietly and wait until the Lord works mystically and inexplicably from on high in order to move you to repentance. If this were the case, I would not have written this book in order to persuade you to love the Sabbath day and to keep it carefully and joyfully to the glory of God. It is vital to hold at least three factors in view.

First, you must recognize that you have already died to the power of sin. God has promised in His Word that if you are in Christ, sin shall not have dominion over you. Christ Jesus came to set you free, not only from the guilt of sin but from the power of sin. He came to destroy the works of the devil (1 John 3:8). Does your faith rest upon these promises in order to repent and obey? Do you take comfort from them in your pursuit of holiness? The Christian must never find himself in a position in which he does not begin and end with the promises of God. This led D. M. Lloyd-Jones to say: "The essence of the Christian position is that you should remind yourself of what you are."[9]

---

9. D. Martyn Lloyd-Jones, *Spiritual Depression: Its Causes and Its Cure* (Grand Rapids: Eerdmans, 2000), 86.

Second, you must pray that God would fulfill these promises in your practice. You must not simply pray, you must be reverently insistent, even humbly demanding, in your prayers. It is irreverence of the highest kind to doubt the exceedingly great and precious promises of God toward you with respect to your sanctification. If you truly believe these things and if you pray in this manner, how can you not labor for holiness with greater earnestness?

Third, you must labor by faith in the promises of God for all you are worth, giving to God all of the glory, praise, and honor for all that is good in you. You must work out your salvation with fear and trembling because it is God who works in you to will and to do of His good pleasure (Phil. 2:12–13). Though you labor more abundantly than all others, you must say with Paul, "Yet not I, but the grace of God which was with me" (1 Cor. 15:10). If you strive to keep the Sabbath, or any other of the commandments of God, without clinging to these vital principles, you will fall into a slavish and legal frame of mind. This will be true whether you adopt the position on Sabbath-keeping represented in the Westminster Standards or not. Whether your ethical standard exceeds the law of God, falls short of it, or agrees with it, sanctification by the works of the law without the continual exercise of faith in the grace of God through Jesus Christ will make you a legalist.

What Is the Solution?

What if you discovered that two people with opposite personalities were actually twins? They appear very different in many respects, but it does not take long to see the family resemblance. It is sometimes asserted that legalism and antinomianism[10] are polar opposites of each other. Some even act as though we can achieve a balanced view regarding the application of the law by taking the legalist's concern for the law, and then adding a dash of the antinomian's rejection of

---

10. Antinomianism means "against law" (*anti* and *nomos*). A legalist abuses the law, either in whole or in part. An antinomian rejects the use of the law as a rule of life, either in whole or in part.

the law in order to mitigate the precision and strictness of the law. This is entirely wrong. Though it may surprise you, legalism and antinomianism are twins who share the same nature. Legalism and antinomianism are not opposites of each other, but are the opposite of God's free grace in Christ.[11] A proper understanding of the manner in which the grace of the gospel transforms our relationship to the law of God is the only true remedy to all abuses of that law.

It is fair to say that antinomianism is actually a subspecies of legalism. Both antinomianism and legalism operate upon a legalistic conception of the relationship between the law and the gospel. Both positions fail to distinguish between the law of God itself and the manner in which the law is used. As we saw in the last chapter, the law of God as summarized in the Ten Commandments is a reflection of the infinitely great and glorious character of the triune God. The law cannot cease making its demands upon God's creatures without God altering His immutable character. Both legalism and antinomianism share the problem that they treat the law as though its only purpose is to serve as a covenant of works, designed to make men acceptable to God. Both suffer from a preoccupation with the effects of the law upon fallen man, rather than the law as a reflection of the God who loved His people and gave His only Son so that they might live through Him by the operation of the Spirit. Both undermine or ignore the significant manner in which the grace of God in the gospel changes our relationship to the law. Neither position places enough trust in the grace of God. The legalist does not place enough trust in the grace of God because he places some trust in himself; the antinomian does not place enough trust in the grace of God because he does not trust God to sanctify him as much as he does to justify him. The legalist willingly places himself under a yoke of bondage; the antinomian casts off the law because he cannot view it as anything other than a yoke of bondage.

11. I am indebted to Sinclair Ferguson's thought-provoking analysis of Thomas Boston and the Marrow Controversy in eighteenth-century Scotland for this observation. His lectures on the Marrow Controversy can be found under that title at www.sermonaudio.com.

The remedy both to legalism and antinomianism, therefore, is the free grace of God in Jesus Christ. The grace of God to us through the covenant of grace established in Christ's blood should lead us to love and cherish the law of God. There are at least two ways in which the gospel has dramatically transformed our relationship to the moral law of God as summarized in the Ten Commandments.

First, we must love the law of God because we love the God of the law. If Christ redeemed a people from sin and wrath in order to care nothing about the holy law of God, this would involve the absurdity that Christ redeemed and gave them His Holy Spirit so they could be indifferent to or despise the character of His heavenly Father. Does not the natural Son love the Father more than He loves the adopted children? If He did not, He would not be the spotless Lamb of God, and He could not take away the sins of the world. In addition to this, what law did Christ keep? Was it not the law of God in all of its perfections? This means that the law of God is not only a reflection of the glory of God the Father, but also a transcript of the life and character of God the Son. As previously quoted, Chantry asserts, "The life of our Lord Jesus Christ was the first biographical inscription of the Moral Law."[12] When the Word became flesh and dwelt among us, it was as though the law became flesh and was illustrated among us. When we study the moral law of God we study the moral character of our beloved Savior, and when we study the character of our Savior we are given greater clarity with regard to the scope of the moral law. What better way to know more of the glory and the beauty of Christ than to study the law of God! To neglect, ignore, or despise the law therefore is to neglect, ignore, or despise Christ Himself. This is like saying, "I love the Lord Jesus Christ, but I am uninterested in who He is," or "I love the Lord Jesus Christ, but I do not love His character." How is it possible, then, to love the Lord Jesus Christ without loving the law of God? You cannot relegate yourself to the commandments contained in the New Testament in this respect, since the New Testament does not con-

12. Chantry, *God's Righteous Kingdom*, 78.

tain the full measure of the moral law, which Christ kept on your behalf as your Redeemer. If it is impossible to love the Lord Jesus Christ without loving the law of God, then it is equally impossible to love the law of God without it greatly affecting your life personally. Do you not see why the law of God is not only relevant to the life of the Christian, but integral to every aspect of his life?[13]

The second solution to confusion regarding our relationship to the moral law is to recognize that law-keeping is one of the provisions of the covenant of grace. The prophet Ezekiel promised that with the coming of the Lord Jesus Christ and the new covenant, God would place His law in the hearts of His people so they would keep it (Ezek. 11:19–20; 36:26–27). Jeremiah referred to this as a new "writing" of the law, and he set it in contrast with the writing of the law of God on the tablets of stone at Mount Sinai. Instead of the law being written upon tablets of stone, it would be written upon men's hearts (Jer. 31:32–33). This is not a different law, but rather the same law that was written upon Adam's heart and published on Mount Sinai. Gradually and progressively, although always imperfectly in this life, those who have been purchased with the blood of Christ have the moral law inscribed upon their hearts. The great commands for godly living in the New Testament are, "Be ye followers of God, as dear children" (Eph. 5:1), and "Be ye holy, for I am holy" (1 Pet. 1:16). God has chosen us in Christ, and He has given us His Holy Spirit so we may be conformed to the image of His Son (Rom. 8:29). The image of the Son is the image of the Father as revealed in the moral law and particularly in the Ten Commandments. The moral law of God is not merely *preparatory* to the covenant of grace (much less contrary to it); the moral law is *integral* to the lives of those who live under the covenant of grace. You cannot be a New Testament believer without being renewed in the image of God in knowledge, righteousness, and holiness (Col. 3:10; Eph. 4:24). If

---

13. For an excellent treatment of Jesus Christ as the pattern for sanctification in relation to the moral law, see John Murray, "The Pattern of Sanctification," in *Collected Writings*, 2:305–12.

Christians better understood the purposes of God in the covenant of grace, they would not question the relevance of the moral law of God in all of its detail. We must love the law in all of its perfections and intricate details, even as we must love the Lord Jesus Christ and be imitators of God with all that is in us, as specifically as possible and in every area of life. We must treat the law as a rare jewel that we hold up to the light and view from every angle in order to take in all of its beauty. Through the law we behold the beauty of the triune God and the glory of Christ. While the law has not changed, our relation to it has changed. The law is just as precise and holy as it ever was. The law applies to every thought and word and action as much as it ever has. Instead of being an oppressive burden to sinners and a continual reminder of wrath, it has become a map to guide the paths of believers in every area of life. There is no area of thought, imagination, speech, or action where the law of God does not shed its light and prepare the way before us

In short, it is only the believer in Christ who can say, "O how love I thy law! It is my meditation all the day" (Ps. 119:97). It is only the Christian who can say that the law is holy, just, and good. It is only the Christian who can say, "I delight in the law of God after the inward man" (Rom. 7:22). No man or woman in either the Old Testament or New Testament could say such things from the standpoint of being under the judgment and condemnation of the law. Only those who have been delivered from the wrath of God demanded by the transgression of His law know the glorious liberty of the sons of God—the freedom to walk in paths of loving and joyful obedience to God's law. Before you are tempted to dismiss a careful and particular view of Sabbath observance, or you are tempted to label that view as legalistic, you must ask yourself whether you have properly grasped the role and place of the law in God's plan of redemption. The covenant of works was added to the original purpose of the law in man's natural condition. The law as a schoolmaster to drive men to Christ is relevant for sinners only; it was not the *original* intent of the law. The moral law of God as a rule of life is the most fundamental and primary purpose of the law. The gospel has placed us in a position where the purpose of the law can be finally restored.

Conclusions

How then should we regard the Sabbath day? We should expect the Scriptures to present a view of the Sabbath that makes it easy to keep. Is the treatment of the fourth commandment in the Westminster Standards truly "legalism"? Not if the only grounds for the accusation are that it is part moral law, that it is a part of the Old Testament, or that it is too strict. We should expect the requirements of Sabbath-keeping to be perfection and to be impossible for sinners to achieve in this life. If this were not so, it could not be part of the perfect and holy law of God. We must not strive to keep the Sabbath in our own strength but rather in dependence upon the Holy Spirit and in longing for the time when we will worship and serve God eternally without weakness or sin. How then must we regard the promises attached to the Sabbath day? How can those who have no hope of fulfilling all that God requires in order to keep the Sabbath day holy expect to lay hold of the promises held forth by God respecting the day? The answer to this question is similar to the manner in which we must examine ourselves in coming to the Lord's Supper. Some people examine themselves and find so much sin that they feel the Supper is not for them. They are unworthy. Yet we must always remember that the promises of the gospel are held forth in the Lord's Supper. Can you ever be made worthy of the gospel promises? Does not this very idea implicitly overthrow the gospel? You must lay hold of Christ by faith. You must examine yourself to the end that you cast yourself upon His mercy and bask in the glory of His grace. You must be transformed by that grace so you have a real hatred for your sins. How can you love what is so contrary to your Savior? What more could motivate you to love righteousness and to love the law of God? The Lord's Supper gives you the assurance and the grace necessary to walk worthy of the calling to which you have been called. The promises attached to the Lord's Day must be approached in the same manner. If you recognize your own weakness and unworthiness, and your faith rests upon God's willingness to richly bless His people in fulfilling His promises, you are on your way to receiving the rich blessings of grace He has attached to the Sabbath day.

The charge of "legalism" that is often leveled against those who carefully set the whole Sabbath apart for the solemn worship of God has unearthed some important questions relating to how we understand the relationship between the law and the gospel in general. Has your objection against keeping the Sabbath been on the basis that this teaching rests primarily on the Old Testament? Does not the character of the Lord Jesus Christ rest greatly on the Old Testament? Do you believe that under the grace of the gospel you do not need to be concerned with law? How can you understand the gospel without the law? How can you love the Savior without loving the law? Do you object to keeping the Sabbath as a day of worship, even in your thoughts and speech, on the grounds that this commandment is too "strict"? Which of the commandments of God are not specific and particular in their application to every aspect of your life? One of the great strengths of historic Protestantism has been its emphasis upon joyful godly living based on obedience to the law of God. The law was regarded as the source of guidance and direction for believers in every area of life. The law was the foundation of the gospel, since it lay at the heart of Christ's atoning work. The law was the only pattern for sanctification the New Testament church knew, since believers were viewed as being renewed in the image of God after the pattern of Jesus Christ.

Beware how you use the term "legalism." Are you legitimately responding to an abuse of the principles of the law of God, or have you distorted the importance God has attached to the law in every stage of redemptive history? It is fearful that the charge of legalism against the careful application of the law of God often reflects the fact that some contemporary Reformed churches have strayed from their biblical and historical roots in the manner in which they understand the relationship between the law and the gospel, the nature of the law itself, and the place of the law within the gospel. A low view of the law—which does not require careful obedience to the law in thought, word, and deed—does not represent a high view of the gospel. On the contrary, failing to apply the law carefully in all of its particulars reflects a low view of grace. The warning that J. C. Ryle gave to the church in his own day is equally relevant today: "There is little danger of men keeping the Sabbath too strictly. The thing to be feared is the disposition to keep it loosely and partially, or not to keep it at all. The tendency of the age is not to exaggerate the fourth commandment, but to cut it out of the Decalogue and to throw it aside altogether. Against this tendency it becomes us all to be on our guard. The experience of eighteen centuries applies abundant proof that vital religion never flourishes where the Sabbath is not well kept."[14] May God grant that this book would accomplish far more in furthering the cause of Christ than merely causing some to rethink the Lord's Day! Oh, that God would grant His people rediscovery of the beauty of His law through the lenses of the new covenant!

---

14. J. C. Ryle, *Expository Thoughts on John* (1869; repr., Edinburgh: Banner of Truth, 1987), 1:280.

CHAPTER TEN

The Eternal Sabbath

If a man spent one-seventh of his life in a foreign culture, eventually aspects of that culture would become indistinguishable from his own customs, clothing, speech, and thoughts. He could not return to his own country without weaving something foreign into all he said and did. We ought to regard the Sabbath in the same manner. By virtue of our citizenship in heaven, we are pilgrims and strangers on the earth. On the Lord's Day, our transactions should be almost exclusively with the heavenly country to which we belong. As we engage in the joys of worship for one whole day in seven, we will live in this world, bringing something "foreign" into everything we do. If heaven consists primarily of communion with God, then to the extent that we enjoy communion with God on earth, we have already begun to enjoy the glories of heaven.[1] On the Sabbath day, God has commanded us to spend the whole day in heaven, so to speak. While we are at home in the body, we are absent from the Lord (2 Cor. 5:6). We have not yet received our permanent dwelling place in our eternal homeland, yet on the Sabbath God allows us to visit heaven and return to this world with the glory of His presence shining from our faces.

It is common to connect the Sabbath to the hope of heaven. Most treatments of the Lord's Day, including those that argue that the Sabbath has been fulfilled in Christ and is no longer in force,

---

1. Burroughs, *Earthly Mindedness*, 20–21.

connect its significance to the hope of glory.[2] However, the connection between the Sabbath and the hope of glory must not be limited to the fact that the Sabbath foreshadows and points to the joys of heaven. The biblical picture of heaven must, as far as possible, serve as the pattern for Sabbath-keeping. In order to establish this vital but often neglected point, I will examine the connection between the Sabbath and the eternal rest of heaven, the activities the Scriptures attach to the eternal rest of heaven, and the manner in which we should use the Sabbath to help us anticipate and long for the eternal rest of heaven.[3] The true glory and beauty of the Sabbath day lie in the fact that when we set apart the day for the corporate and private worship of God, we partake in the primary joys of heaven. Because the Sabbath is a type or shadow of heaven, our earthly Sabbaths are designed to be the closest reflection in this life of the glory that will be revealed in the life to come. This is the highest reason the Sabbath must be a day of sacred rest consisting of worship.

The Eternal Rest

In Scripture, the Sabbath is inseparably connected to the hope of heaven. The classic passage that connects the day to the believer's hope of eternal rest is Hebrews 4:1–11. The arguments presented in this text are highly complex and intricate. I do not intend to examine the passage in detail here, nor do I desire to improve upon the exegesis of other more capable scholars. By providing a brief overview of the general thrust of the argument, my goal is simply to establish the inseparable connection between Sabbath-keeping and the hope of our eternal rest in heaven.[4]

---

2. This is why some people believe that the Sabbath is no longer in force, since Christ has secured the promise of heaven for believers. See appendix 2 in this book .

3. One notable exception to this neglect is the last chapter of Iain Campbell's *First Day of the Week*. Campbell lists six characteristics about heaven that should serve as the pattern for Sabbath-keeping. I have sought to avoid overlap with his material by utilizing different arguments from this chapter.

4. Richard Gaffin has furnished the church with two excellent expositions

The author of the book of Hebrews wrote to Jewish Christians who were being pressured to return to the ceremonies, sacrifices, and customs of Judaism. He vehemently denounced such a return as apostasy from Christ and a denial of the grace of the gospel. For this reason, the book of Hebrews progresses through cycles of threats against those turning away from Christ, followed by glorious and majestic statements of the surpassing excellence and superiority of Christ over the ordinances of worship of Judaism. Christ is the end, fulfillment, and sole purpose of the entire Old Testament priesthood, worship, and sacrifices. It is in this context and with these emphases that the author begins his discussion of the purpose of the Sabbath day.

Hebrews 4 begins with an exhortation to Jewish believers to be diligent to enter the promised rest of God, reminding them that only those who believe in the Lord Jesus Christ will enter that rest (vv. 1–3). The author then reminds them that this rest was first promised in the institution of the Sabbath day, on the seventh day following the creation of the world (v. 4). In other words, at the very inception of creation, the primary design of the Sabbath was to present mankind with an eschatological hope.[5] The example of God's resting on the seventh day is treated as an implicit promise or pledge that mankind should enjoy this eternal rest with God. Yet the people under the Old Testament did not enter into that rest, since Psalm 95 (ascribed to David) threatened that the disobedient would not enter

---

of this passage, which helps the reader to digest the content of Hebrews 4 carefully. Gaffin also provides useful responses to much of the modern literature that has been written against the continuing relevance of the Sabbath day. See Richard Gaffin, "A Sabbath Rest Still Awaits the People of God," in *Pressing Toward the Mark: Essays Commemorating Fifty Years of the Orthodox Presbyterian Church* (Philadelphia: The Committee for the Historian of the Orthodox Presbyterian Church, 1986), 33–52; and "Westminster and the Sabbath," in *The Westminster Confession into the 21st Century* (Geanies House, U.K.: Christian Focus Publications, 2003), 123–44.

5. For an excellent discussion of the eschatological promises implied by the institution of the Sabbath, see Geerhardus Vos, *The Eschatology of the Old Testament* (Phillipsburg, N.J.: P&R, 2001), 73–76.

into that rest in the future. By the time of King David, this Sabbath rest was a pledge and still remained a future promise. It should be noted that after the Fall, in order for the Sabbath to continue to be a relevant pledge of rest, it not only referred to the pledge of rest in creation, but also to a pledge secured by redemption. This was why the reference to the exodus from Egypt was added in Deuteronomy 5:15 as a reason for Sabbath-keeping. The exodus itself was a pledge that God would ultimately redeem His people through the person and work of the Lord Jesus Christ. As Roland Ward argued, appealing to the exodus was not so much an additional reason for keeping the Sabbath as a foreshadowing of the means by which the original purpose of the Sabbath at creation would be restored.[6] It is only through faith in Christ as the Redeemer that we have hope of entering into God's eternal rest. This fact, however, became clear in Scripture only through the gradual process of redemptive history. The eschatological promise attached to the Sabbath in creation and secured by redemption stands behind the arguments of Hebrews 4.

Implicit throughout this chapter is the assumption that the "rest" of God into which believers must enter is permanent in duration. This rest was promised by the Sabbath at creation, and it continued to be relevant because of the work Christ would accomplish. By the time David wrote Psalm 95, the promise of entering God's rest still loomed ahead in the distance. Lest Jewish Christians be deceived by looking to the conquest of Canaan for the fulfillment of God's promises, the author reminded them that Joshua did not bring them into God's rest by conquering the land (v. 8). God's people cannot enter into God's rest by striving to return to the Old Testament way of life in the land of Canaan. Instead they must look to the future rest, which has been secured by Christ alone. This was the future hope alluded to by David in the psalm. The argument of the chapter continues: if the promise of entering into God's rest remains for the future, then God's people must look forward, not back, in order to enter that rest.

---

6. Ward, "Sabbath," 197.

Every argument in this epistle focuses on the necessity of entering into the presence of God through the Lord Jesus Christ alone. This section is no different. God had promised eternal rest to His people; that rest did not come through Joshua. The promise remains for the future, and the hope of entering God's rest comes only through Jesus Christ. This rest that comes through Jesus Christ was likely what the author had in mind when he wrote: "For he that is entered into his rest, he also hath ceased from his own works, as God did from his" (v. 10). Just as God gave a pledge of eternal rest to His people when He rested from the works of creation, so Jesus Christ secured this rest when He ceased or rested from His works of redemption. The rest of Christ, therefore, is compared to the rest of God in its magnitude and secures this rest for His people with unshakable certainty.[7] In fact, the work of Christ excels the work of creation in that it not only restores man's hope of eternal rest with the eternally majestic and glorious triune God, but it does so in a more glorious manner than if man had never fallen into sin! The hope of every Christian rests securely on the words of Christ on the cross: "It is finished!" (John 19:30). Christ completed His work of redemption just as God did His work of creation, so that all who are weary and heavy laden are given the promise of eternal rest for their souls, if they will only come to Him.

Verse 9 is the pivotal verse in this section. The author argues that in light of all he has said there still remains a rest (*sabbatismos*) for the people of God. This is an unusual term, and it differs from the other word translated as "rest" in this chapter. The *sabbatismos*

---

7. Gaffin argues on grammatical grounds that the pronoun "he" in this passage should refer to the believer entering into God's eternal rest rather than to Christ resting from his work. However, it seems more consistent with the context and with the manner of argumentation in the book of Hebrews to root and ground all of his exhortations in the finished work of Christ. Verse 10 contains the indicative statement that provides the hope and encouragement to fulfill the imperative of verse 11. For criticism of Gaffin's position, see Pipa, *Lord's Day*, 119–22. For a thorough exegesis of the position I have presented, see Owen, *Day of Sacred Rest*, 411ff.

most likely refers to the hope of keeping Sabbath with God in eternity. This interpretation is reinforced by the exhortation of verse 11: "Let us labour therefore to enter into *that* rest, lest any man fall after the same example of unbelief" (emphasis added).[8] Many authors have understood this term to refer here to the Christian Sabbath, which we must continue to keep as a pledge of God's eternal rest. Even if this is not what is immediately asserted in the passage, it is an inescapable implication of the text. The use of the term *sabbatismos* inextricably connects Sabbath-keeping with the hope of glory. Our heavenly rest *is* keeping an eternal Sabbath, and our earthly Sabbaths hold forth the promise of this heavenly rest. Not to have an earthly Sabbath, while the promise of entering God's rest lies in the future, is inconceivable. As believers, even though our hope of heaven is as secure as if we were already there, the fact remains that we have not yet entered into that rest. We must wait patiently for it, and we must persevere in expectation of it through faith in Christ's finished work. From creation until consummation, there shall always be a Sabbath on earth to help the saints long to keep the Sabbath in heaven. It is only natural in this connection that the apostles, under divine guidance, should have occupied the day of Christ's resurrection with acts of religious worship. As Owen wisely noted, if the example of God in completing the work of creation was sufficient to set apart the seventh day, then the example of Christ in completing the work of redemption was sufficient to change the Sabbath to the first day of the week.[9]

Many lessons ought to be drawn from this passage. The primary point in this connection, however, is that the concept of keeping the Sabbath day is inseparably tied to the hope of our eternal rest in heaven. The Sabbath is designed to be a shadow of heavenly realities. Just as the Lord's Supper foreshadows the day when we will sit down at the wedding feast of the Lamb with Abraham and the patriarchs,

---

8. "Unbelief" should be translated "disobedience" in order to be more faithful to the Greek text.

9. Owen, *Day of Sacred Rest*, 409–10.

together with all who are called from the four corners of the earth, so the Sabbath continues to foreshadow our hope of communion with God and His church in heaven. A church without a Sabbath is a church that implicitly relinquishes its hope of heaven. Just as a shadow depends upon a body for its shape and not vice versa, so the picture of the eternal Sabbath should provide the pattern and shape of our earthly Sabbaths.

The Activities of the Eternal Rest

William Plumer made this astute observation: "No man on earth knows much of heaven."[10] The Puritan Thomas Manton added, "Heavenly joys cannot be told us in an earthly dialect; the Scripture is fain to lisp to us, and speak as we can understand, of things to come by things present; therefore our glory is in great measure unknown, and will be till we get up and see what a crown of glory is prepared for us."[11] In light of the large amount of speculation that often occurs concerning the activities of the saints in heaven, this is a vital reminder. We do not yet know what we shall be. When Christ appears we shall be like Him because we shall see Him as He is (1 John 3:1–2). Our corrupt mortal bodies will be transformed into the image of His incorrupt and immortal body (Phil. 3:21; 1 Cor. 15:49). Although we know little about the activities of heaven, it is clear that virtually the only activity explicitly connected with heaven in Scripture is the worship of God. If the earthly Sabbath is patterned after the heavenly Sabbath, then the little that has been revealed about our eternal state should play an important role in how we keep the Sabbath.[12]

---

10. William S. Plumer, *Theology for the People* (New York: The American Tract Society, 1875; repr., Harrisonburg, Va.: Sprinkle Publications, 2005), 214.

11. Thomas Manton, *The Complete Works of Thomas Manton*, ed. A. B. Grossart (London: J. Nisbet, 1870), 20:457.

12. For an outstanding exposition of the biblical teaching on heaven, see Edward Donnelly, *Biblical Teaching on the Doctrines of Heaven and Hell* (Edinburgh: Banner of Truth, 2001).

Seeing and Worshiping God

Even with the disadvantage of trying to comprehend the incomprehensible eternal glory of the world to come, the basic biblical picture of heaven is fairly straightforward. The activity of heaven can be legitimately summarized in one word: *worship*. It is not much of an overstatement to use "eternal worship" as a synonym for heaven. Worship on earth is heaven begun; worship in glory is heaven perfected. The reason for this is that there is nothing more worthy of our attention and more satisfying to our natures than the glory of the Trinity. When the apostle Paul was taken up into what he called "the third heaven" (2 Cor. 12:2), he heard "unspeakable [inexpressible] words, which it is not lawful for man to utter" (v. 4). God told His servant Moses that no man could see Him and live (Ex. 33:20). This limitation placed upon man is not exclusive to the Old Testament and continues in the New Testament. The apostle John wrote, "No man hath seen God at any time. The only begotten Son, which is in the bosom of the Father, he hath declared him" (John 1:18; see 1 John 4:12).[13] Even Paul in his transportation into "the third heaven" had neither the privilege nor the ability to see God in His unveiled majesty, since he later wrote that God "only hath immortality, dwelling in the light which no man can approach unto; *whom no man hath seen, nor can see*" (1 Tim. 6:16, emphasis added).[14] Even the sinless angels in heaven veil their faces in the sight of the majesty of God (Isa. 6:2). Sinful creatures cannot behold the radiance of His glory and survive the encounter. The infinite, eternal, and unchangeable Maker of heaven and earth is above all blessing and praise. He is great and greatly to be praised, and His greatness is unsearchable. Yet Christ promised that the "pure in heart" shall see God (Matt. 5:8). When we see Him as He is and stand in the presence of a being of such infinite worth and unfathomable glory, what

---

13. There is strong textual evidence that the word "Son" here should actually be "God," which emphasizes that the one who came and declared the glory of God was Himself the one and only God in human flesh.

14. In the context, it is interesting that this text actually refers to *Christ*.

else could attract our attention? How could we ever be distracted or "bored" in the presence of God?[15] Even apart from considering our fall into sin and the redemption purchased by Christ, it is difficult to see how a sinless creature could possibly desire anything in heaven other than to explore God's infinite glory and beauties, worshiping Him more and more with every wondrous discovery.

How much more will redeemed sinners have cause to be consumed with the worship of God in heaven! The greatness of redemption and the full realization of the magnitude of the debt we owed due to sin, coupled with the wonder of the Father's love toward us in Christ, will utterly consume us when we enter into heaven. The precise details of heaven may be somewhat hazy, yet it is beyond doubt that joyful worship will set the tone for eternity. Revelation 4 and 5 illustrate this beyond doubt. In chapter 4, God is introduced as sitting upon His throne with all the host of heaven praising Him for His holiness and the creation of all things (Rev. 4:8, 11). At this stage in the unfolding picture, John wrote, "And *they rest not day and night*, saying, Holy, holy, holy, LORD God Almighty, which was, and is, and is to come" (v. 8, emphasis added). In chapter 5, this scene of exuberant worship reaches its peak when the Lord Jesus Christ enters the scene. When He opens the scroll of God, the four living creatures and the twenty-four elders burst forth into praise (Rev. 5:8–10). They are soon joined by an innumerable multitude of angels surrounding the throne (v. 11). As the thunder of these mighty voices spreads in praise to Jesus Christ, "every creature which is in heaven, and on the earth" (v. 13) joins the chorus. If the angels praise the Lamb for His work in redeeming lost human beings, how could we who have been cleansed by the blood of the Lamb be consumed with anything other than eternal praise and

---

15. Paul Helm argues that there will be no boredom in heaven because there will be a continual increase of creative activity on the part of man. However likely this may be, we do not have to go beyond the marvels of the glory of the triune God to explain why the redeemed shall never tire of heaven. See Paul Helm, *The Last Things: Death, Judgment, Heaven, and Hell* (Edinburgh: Banner of Truth, 1989), 95.

worship? The extent to which we fail to understand why we would desire nothing other than worship in heaven reflects the proportion to which we have failed to understand the glory and wonder of the grace of the Trinity in the gospel. If you are in Christ, there will come a day in which you will be made like Christ, and being made like Him you will finally see Him as He is (1 John 3:2). If you have any doubt that it will take eternity to express your gratitude to the triune God, that doubt will be removed when you arrive there.

Other Activities in Heaven
Many Christians probably think implicitly of heaven in terms of a place where redeemed souls go when they depart from the body at death. This, however, is only the beginning of heaven. Ultimately, heaven will be a place where the Lord Jesus Christ will reverse the effects of the Fall. After removing His enemies and casting them into the lake of fire, the Lord will inaugurate a world in which "all things" are reconciled to Himself (Col. 1:20). We must not think about heaven as a place for incorporeal ethereal beings. The bodies of those who are in Christ will rest in their graves until the resurrection, when they will be raised after the image of Christ's glorious body (Phil. 3:21). These bodies will have an environment suited to their nature. Paul describes the present world, not as being annihilated, but as being resurrected in a manner comparable to the resurrection of our own bodies (Rom. 8).[16] This means there will be some degree of continuity between this life and the life to come. This has led many to speculate about the continuation of various activities that men enjoyed upon earth, such as reading classical literature and even continuing in ordinary labor.

I cannot reject such notions absolutely, since we know so little about the life to come, but perhaps I am even less comfortable

---

16. Since this is not the appropriate place to discuss various views of the eternal state, for a useful treatment of the relevant passages in which the earth is restored at the second coming of Christ rather than destroyed see, Joseph A. Pipa and David W. Hall, *Did God Create in 6 Days?* (Greenville, S.C.: Southern Presbyterian Press, 1999).

accepting them. While it is true that the Scriptures teach that this world will be redeemed and that its pre-Fall purposes will be restored, we also must not underestimate how different things will be in the eternal state. This is illustrated well by considering the relevance of creation ordinances in eternity. Creation ordinances continue to be relevant in eternity, but they will be expressed very differently. Redemption and eternity will transform every creation ordinance. Marriage will not continue as we know it (Matt. 22:30), but will give place to the marriage supper of the Lamb (Rev. 19:6–9; 21:9). In heaven, the weekly Sabbath will become obsolete because heaven itself will be the Sabbath. What about the creation ordinance of labor? By analogy to the other creation ordinances, the ordinance of labor will likely have some continuing relevance in eternity. Yet as with the other creation ordinances, labor is likely to resemble only vaguely its earthly counterpart. How can any form of ordinary labor be consistent in a state of eternal Sabbath-keeping when the earthly Sabbath excluded it? Will labor and Sabbath-keeping ultimately become the same act as worship becomes the sole labor of the saints in glory? Does this not illustrate that these are things of which we know little to nothing about? We will be certain only when we get there. Whatever is actually true about heaven, the old idea of heaven consisting of the beatific vision, or the sight of God, seems to be basically correct.[17] It is clear that whatever else might be true about heaven, the clear picture God has painted in Scripture is one

---

17. For an excellent exposition of the traditional "beatific vision" view of heaven, see Jonathan Edwards, "The Pure in Heart Blessed," in *Works*, 905–12. The only hesitation I have with Edwards's treatment of heaven in this sermon is that he tends to undermine and neglect the physical at points. He argues that the saints will not see God with the physical eye, but only with the eye of the heart. Edwards went beyond many of the earlier Puritans in this regard by treating matter as though it did not belong to true reality. At points, Edwards advocated an almost Platonic "typology" in which spiritual realities were treated almost as the only true realities. For an insightful analysis of Edwards on this point, see John Carrick, *Preaching of Jonathan Edwards*, 194–99. In contrast to Edwards, Manton wrote that part of the joy of seeing God in heaven must be "ocular…for our senses have their happiness as well as

of unceasing and eternal worship of the triune God. If the Sabbath is meant to set forth the hope of heaven and serve as a dim earthly picture of a bright eternal glory, then on our earthly Sabbaths we should strive to be consumed with worship in a manner that agrees with this depiction.

The Other-Worldly Character of the Christian Life
Once again, the manner in which we regard the Sabbath day unearths more vital problems. The counterpart to Sabbath-breaking as a symptom of worldliness is that Sabbath-breaking is a symptom of either a shift in focus away from the life to come, or of distorted views of what God has revealed about the life to come. This has the highest possible significance for how we live our lives in this world. As John Carrick wrote, "The essentially other-worldly character of the Christian faith has, especially from the latter part of the nineteenth century onwards, been eroded; and it has been replaced by an essentially this-worldly interpretation. Thus the focus in much modern theology falls, increasingly, upon man at the expense of God and upon this life and this world at the expense of the life and the world to come."[18] This is not to say that everyone who does not view the Sabbath as a day set apart for worship is ungodly or has abandoned the hope of heaven, but the fact is that the church's views of heaven and the life to come have shifted dramatically over the course of the past century. The corresponding decline in Sabbath-keeping is only an inevitable reflection of this fact. When the church's primary hope is to see Christ face to face in heaven and to worship Him in His unveiled glory, this great and central hope will be the dominant feature of her members. The one day that God has designed to foreshadow heaven on earth will inevitably reflect this fact. If our primary hope is set on the life to come, and if we believe

their souls." *Complete Works*, 20:460. Nevertheless, Edwards's description of the believer's delight in beholding the glory of God is without parallel.
18. John Carrick, *The Preaching of Jonathan Edwards* (Edinburgh: Banner of Truth), 118.

that the primary joy and privilege of that life is worship and communion with God, then our earthly Sabbaths should imitate the heavenly realities as much as is possible.

If the other-worldly character of the Christian life is being eroded, it is partly because men have adopted a this-worldly view of heaven.[19] This is a subtle and dangerous distortion of the truth, since some men deceive themselves with a hope that is essentially worldly in the name of a Christianity that justifies and encourages such a hope. Our forefathers in the faith used to warn men that one test of hypocrisy was the manner in which people conceived heaven. If they did not find their greatest joy and longing in the hope that they would worship God without sin, it was unlikely that they truly understood and laid hold of the gospel. For the same reason, they gave the same warning to those who found no enjoyment in the worship and activities of the Sabbath. As Plumer noted, "The Sabbath is, and in Scripture is made to be, a type of the glorious rest of the people of God in heaven. If men do not relish the type, it is proof positive that they are not prepared for the antitype. Let us all diligently ask for grace to prepare us for 'employments, the society and worship of that Sabbath which remains for the people of God.'"[20] The case is even worse when the duties of the day and the use of the means of grace simply become burdensome. Owen warned:

> He who really judgeth in his mind, and whose practice is influenced and regulated by that judgment, that the segregation of a day from the world and the occasions of it, and a secession

---

19. Richard Gaffin has asserted that the Westminster position on the Sabbath gave little attention to eschatology because it gave so much attention to worship. Gaffin, "Westminster and the Sabbath," 142. However, even if the Westminster divines had devoted more attention to the eschatological focus of the Sabbath, they would have come to the same conclusions with respect to Sabbath-keeping because their eschatology was dominated by worship. The fact that the Sabbath should not leave room for activities other than worship does not so much reflect a neglect of eschatology as a different view of eschatology.

20. Plumer, *Law of God*, 341.

unto communion with God thereon, is grievous and burdensome, and that which God doth not require, nor is useful to
us, must be looked upon as a stranger unto these things....
Alas! what would such persons do if they should ever come to
heaven, to be taken aside to all eternity to be with God alone,
who think it a great bondage to be here diverted unto him for
a day?[21]

Many gave similar warnings to those who conceived of heaven in a
manner that was exclusively worldly. William Bates noted:

This one consideration of heaven, that it is a holy rest, is that
which makes it unamiable, and undesirable to carnal men. It
is true, such may desire it as a refuge from hell: but they desire
it not as a state wherein they are to be always conversant in the
love of God, and in the presence of God, and the everlasting
enjoyment of him. Carnal men cannot taste it, they have not
a proper palate for it: it can only draw forth the heart of the
saints: and yet, let me tell you, this is the substantial blessed-
ness of heaven.[22]

Since there is much unknown about heaven, we do not know
what relation we will have to our loved ones who have departed to
be with the Lord. It does seem that we will find joy in their fellowship again, but we do not know in what manner life as we know it
will continue in heaven. We know that we will be body-and-soul
creatures in an environment suited to our physical as well as our
spiritual natures, yet we must always recognize that the focus and
emphasis of heaven is the worship and praise of God. Heaven will be
like a great treasure room in which the greatest treasure of all lies in
the center of the room, and the treasure in the center is so great that
it diverts the attention of all who enter into the room, almost to the
neglect of all else. Yet the wonder and beauty of the treasures that fill

---

21. Owen, *Day of Sacred Rest*, 451.
22. William Bates, *The Everlasting Rest of the Saints in Heaven*, in *The Complete Works of William Bates* (repr., Harrisonburg, Va.: Sprinkle Publications, 1990), 3:21.

the room provide the only appropriate backdrop for this greatest of all treasures; the wealth contained in the room only accentuates the beauty of the centerpiece. We must never forget that God Himself is that great all-consuming treasure of heaven, and that whatever else He has designed to be part of that world will serve only to accentuate His beauty and to drive us to more soul-ravishing worship.

If the Sabbath is inextricably connected to the hope of heaven, then the biblical conception of heaven should shape our Sabbath-keeping. The eternal rest of God those who are in Christ hope to enter will be a rest that is consumed with plumbing the depths of God's infinite attributes and triune nature with increasing joy, wonder, and astonishment over the depths of God's love manifested in Christ. If heaven is consumed with worship, should not our Sabbaths also be consumed with worship? If the worship of God lies at the center of our heavenly rest, should it not also be at the center of our earthly rest? Out of all of the reasons why the Sabbath should be considered as a day sanctified to God for the purpose of worship, this is the highest of all. Do we not enjoy communion with God with difficulty at the present time? Do we not long to enter into the full enjoyment of our God in eternity? The Sabbath is set apart for worship to help promote these ends. Let us test the manner in which we regard the Lord's Day in light of Thomas Boston's description:

> The Sabbath, in the esteem of saints, is the queen of days; and they shall have an endless Sabbatism in the kingdom of heaven, so shall their garments always be white. They will have an eternal rest, with an uninterrupted joy; for heaven is not a resting place, where men may sleep out an eternity; there they rest not day or night, but their work is their rest, and continual recreation, and toil and weariness have no place there. They rest there in God, who is the center of their souls. Here they find the completion, or satisfaction, of all their desires, having the full enjoyment of God, and uninterrupted communion with him. This is the point to which, til the soul come, it will always be restless: but that point reached, it rests; for God is the last end, and the soul can go no further. It cannot understand,

will, nor desire more; but in him it has what is commensurable to its boundless desires.[23]

The Anticipation of the Eternal Rest

When a family plans a vacation, sometimes the children can barely contain their anticipation. If the children know they are going to Walt Disney World for the first time, they can become so excited that all they think about is what it will be like. They look through everything they can find on it, they ask others who know about the place, and they begin to imagine what they will do when they get there. Children tend to be fairly particular about making sure they have meticulously accurate information in such matters.

Too often the simple excitement of a child betrays what little attention we give to our hope of eternal rest with the triune God. We need every help we can get to set our minds upon things above where Christ is, rather than upon things on the earth. The Sabbath day is one of the greatest blessings and helps provided by the Lord in assisting His people to long for the glories of heaven. If we sanctify and love the Sabbath day, we will find that God has filled that day with all of the means necessary to help us in our journey. Here are three ways in which Sabbath-keeping should help you anticipate heaven.

First, *Sabbath-keeping should mimic or imitate the activities of heaven.* Heaven is both the embodied hope and pattern for Sabbath-keeping. In some respects, worldly recreations are even more contrary to the purposes of the Sabbath than worldly employments.[24] At least in our worldly employments we have the excuse of arguing that we are pursuing a legitimate calling that is necessary to sustain our lives in this world, which constitutes a large part of our obedience to God in this life. By pursuing recreations on the Sabbath such as sports and television, however, we implicitly declare that these earthly diversions are more interesting to us than the worship of

---

23. Thomas Boston, *Human Nature in its Fourfold State* (repr., Edinburgh: Banner of Truth, 2002), 441–42.
24. See Dwight, *Theology Explained*, 3:271.

God. Sadly, even the best of the saints on earth know that in some measure this often proves to be the case. We are weak and sinful, and we do not love God or His worship as we ought to. We must recognize our tendency to desire recreation on the day sanctified to the Lord for worship as a significant weakness. By worshiping God in public and private throughout the entire Sabbath day, we will mortify the desires of the flesh and our earthly mindedness more than anything else we do on earth. We should look at Sabbath-keeping as training and practice for the worship we will enjoy in glory.

Second, *Sabbath-keeping should encourage us on our way to heaven*. On earth, God manifests Himself most clearly through the means of grace. These include the reading and especially the preaching of the Word of God, laying hold of the promises of the gospel set forth in the sacraments, and uniting in corporate prayer and fellowship. This is not an exhaustive list of the means by which God communicates His grace to His people, yet these means are some of the most vital ones, and they are a regular part of corporate worship on the Lord's Day. As we have seen, the means of grace are dispensed with the greatest power and effect in corporate worship. It is possible that in heaven we will enjoy corporate worship to the exclusion of private worship. In addition to this, one of the promises attached to Sabbath-keeping is delighting in God (Isa. 58:14). We must come to the Sabbath with the anticipation of travelers who are sightseeing in an exotic foreign land. Only the "sights" that we come to see in Sabbath worship are the glories of God in the face of Jesus Christ (2 Cor. 4:6). The glasses we must use to see these "sights" are God's appointed means by which He communicates His grace to His people.

Third, *the Sabbath should increase faith in God through Jesus Christ*. Most of us know too well the experience of not finding the same glory in corporate worship that the Scriptures attach to it. The primary reason for this is often because we do not actually believe that corporate worship is what Scripture says it is. We receive the blessings contained in the promises of Scripture by trusting that God will fulfill them, and it is by faith alone that we have appropriated the blessing of the gospel of Jesus Christ. We have done so by laying hold of the promises of God in the Word and in the sacraments. The Sabbath should help us long for heaven because it demands that we exercise our faith by laying hold of God through the ordinances of corporate worship. In heaven, we will live by sight and no longer by faith, but on earth we walk by faith and not by sight (2 Cor. 5:7). We need every encouragement to strengthen our faith in the promises of God, especially through using His ordinances. The Sabbath simultaneously requires us to exercise our faith, and it contains promises to strengthen our faith.

If you diligently, prayerfully, and joyfully use the means that God has attached to the Sabbath in order to get the most you can out of the day, I doubt you will have time for your worldly employments or recreations. Rather than longing for the Sabbath to be over, we will be left wondering where the day has gone. This is as it ought to be. If the Sabbath is like a short visit to heaven, then part of the blessing of our earthly Sabbaths is that they end so soon. The temporary rest afforded through the Sabbath should make you long for eternal rest. This does not mean that Sabbath-keeping will not be difficult for believers. Many find it is the most difficult task they have ever set their hands to, especially when they first begin; but you have exceedingly great and precious promises. Look to the Lord in your Sabbath-keeping. He will help you, and He will fulfill His promises. There has never been a word that has proceeded from His mouth that will ever fail.

Conclusions

Every moment we delight in our fellowship and communion with the triune God on earth testifies to the fact that we have already begun to enjoy the highest blessing of glory. God has given us one day in seven on which we may pursue fellowship and communion with Him to the exclusion of all else. The two places in the Bible where man is found in a state of perfection, he is keeping the Sabbath as a day of worship. Both the creation ordinance and the consummated purpose of the Sabbath demonstrate that it is a day in which the entire time is to be taken up in the public and private exercise of God's worship. We must spend every day longing for heaven, yet on one day of the week we are to act as though we are already there. Have we misunderstood the requirements of the fourth commandments because of a misguided hope of heaven? I hope we know better. Yet how then can so many claim to keep the Sabbath with leisure and recreation when heaven is the pattern of it? Just as Christianity was not fashioned after Judaism but Judaism after Christianity,[25] so heaven is not fashioned after Sabbath-keeping but Sabbath-keeping after heaven. If you still view heaven as your own private golf course in the kingdom, you are in for a rude awakening. In light of so many man-centered and shallow views of the life to come, it is not surprising that a commandment forbidding all unnecessary thoughts, words, and works about our worldly employments and recreations is foreign to most. What is surprising is that so many people who long for an eternity of uninterrupted worship and communion with the triune God cannot comprehend why we must exclude these activities from the Sabbath.

The glimpses given in Scripture of the glories of heaven depict the church of the firstborn and of the glorified saints in heaven, along with an innumerable company of angels, worshiping God day and night with purified souls and glorified bodies. Whatever else is true about heaven, this picture of unceasing worship and communion with the great triune Jehovah of Hosts is clearly the focus that He intended to communicate to His church. God seems to have deemed it sufficient for us to view heaven as a place of worship and

---

25. Eadie's description of the relationship between Christianity and Judaism applies equal force to the relationship between heaven and the Sabbath: "The sketch is taken from the reality, and implies the existence of it. The shadow is the intended likeness of the substance. In other words, Christianity was not fashioned to resemble Judaism, but Judaism was fashioned to resemble Christianity. The antitype is not constructed to bear a likeness to the type, but the type is constructed to bear a likeness to the antitype. It is, in short, because of the antitype that the type exists." John Eadie, *Colossians* (1856; repr., Minneapolis: Klock & Klock, 1980), 180.

communion with Himself. A place of eternal worship is the pattern for our earthly Sabbaths. May you know the joys of an eternity with God in heaven by knowing the joys of a day with God on earth. As Thomas Watson exhorted, may you use every Sabbath as though it may be your last:

> When this blessed day approaches, we must lift up our hearts in thankfulness to God that he has put another means into our hands for gaining heavenly wisdom. These are our spiritual harvest days. The wind of God's Spirit blows upon the sails of our affections and we may be carried further in our heavenly voyage. Christian, lift up your heart to God in thankfulness that he has given you another golden season. Be sure you improve it; it may be the last. Seasons of grace are not like the tide: if a man misses one tide, he may have another.[26]

26. Thomas Watson, *Heaven Taken by Storm: Showing the Holy Violence a Christian Is to Put Forth in the Pursuit after Glory*, ed. Joel R. Beeke (Morgan, Pa.: Soli Deo Gloria, 2000), 35.

The Foundations of the Sabbath in the Word of God

B. B. WARFIELD[1]

I am to speak to you today, not of the usefulness or of the blessed-ness of the Sabbath, but of its obligation. And I am to speak to you of its obligation, not as that obligation naturally arises out of its use-fulness or blessedness, but as it is immediately imposed by God in His Word. You naturally dwell on the joy of the Sabbath. This is the day of gladness and triumph, on which the Lord broke the bonds of the grave, abolishing death and bringing life and immortality to light. As naturally you dwell on the value of the Sabbath. This is the day on which the tired body rests from its appointed labor; on which the worn spirit finds opportunity for recuperation; an oasis in the desert of earthly cares, when we can escape for a moment from the treadmill toil of daily life and, at leisure from ourselves, refresh our souls in God. I am to recall your minds—it may seem some-what brusquely—to the contemplation of the duty of the Sabbath; and to ask you to let them rest for a moment on the bald notion of

---

1. I have chosen to append this excellent treatment of the perpetuity of the Sabbath to the end of this book primarily for the benefit of those who do not come to this subject with a prior conviction that the Sabbath is binding upon Christians. This address was initially given at the Fourteenth Inter-national Lord's Day Congress held in Oakland, California, July 27–August 1, 1915. It was published in *Sunday the World's Rest Day* by Duncan James McMilan and Alexander Jackson (Garden City, N.Y.: Doubleday, Page, and Co., 1916), 63–81, and in *The Free Presbyterian Magazine* (Glasgow, 1918), 316–19, 350–54, 378–83, as well as in a pamphlet (Glasgow, 1918). I have added Scripture references in brackets.

authority. I do not admit that, in so doing, I am asking you to lower your eyes. Rather, I conceive myself to be inviting you to raise them; to raise them to the very pinnacle of the pinnacle. After all is said, there is no greater word than "ought." And there is no higher reason for keeping the Sabbath than that I ought to keep it; that I owe it to God the Lord to keep it in accordance with His command.

It may nevertheless require some little effort to withdraw our thoughts even for a moment from the utility of the Sabbath and fix them on its bare obligation. Since [Pierre-Joseph] Proudhon[2] taught the world the natural value of the Sabbath, its supernatural origin and sanction have, in wide circles, passed perhaps somewhat out of sight. In its abounding usefulness to man, it may seem so obviously man's day that we may easily forget that it was for two thousand years before it was discovered to be man's day already the Lord's Day; and, stretching back from that, from the creation of the world God's day. The Sabbath is undoubtedly rooted in nature; in our human nature and in the nature of the created universe. Unbroken toil is not good for us; the recurrence of a day of rest is of advantage to us, physically, mentally, spiritually. But had we been left to find this out for ourselves, we should probably have waited very long for it. Certainly Proudhon tardily learned it from observation, not of pure nature, but of the Sabbath rest ordained by God. We are told on the highest authority that "the Sabbath was made for man" [Mark 2:27]. Man needs it. It blesses his life. But man apparently would never have had it, had it not been "made" for him; made for him by Him who from the beginning of the world has known all His works, and, knowing man, has made for him from the beginning of the world the day of rest which he needs. He who needed no rest, in the greatness of his condescension, rested from the work which He had creatively made, that by His example He might woo man to his needed rest.

---

2. Pierre-Joseph Proudhon (1809–1865), called the father of anarchism, was a French philosopher, journalist, and socialist. He was elected to the Constituent Assembly, and he was the first to call himself an anarchist. He is considered among the most influential of anarchist writers and organizers. *The Encyclopedia of Philosophy*, s.v. "Proudhon, Pierre-Joseph."

The Sabbath, then, is not an invention of man's, but a creation of God's. "This is the day which the LORD hath made" [Ps. 118:24]—a verse than which none in the Psalter has had a more glorious history—does not refer to the Sabbath; but it is not strange that it has been so frequently applied to it that it has ended by becoming on the lips of God's people one of its fixed designations. It is Jehovah who made the Sabbath; though for man, the Sabbath is not of man, but has come to man as a gift from God Himself. And, as God has made it, so He has kept it, as He has kept all else that He has made, under His own hand. It is in the power of no man to unmake the Sabbath, or to remake it—diverting it from, or, as we might fondly hope, adjusting it better to, its divinely appointed function. What God has made it, that will He Himself see that it shall remain. This in effect our Savior tells us in that very saying to which we have already alluded. For, immediately upon declaring that "the Sabbath was made for man"—with the open implication, of course, that it was by God that it was made for man—he proceeds to vindicate to himself the sole empire over it. "So that," he adds, "the Son of Man is Lord even of the Sabbath" [Mark 2:28].

The little word "even" should not pass unobserved in this declaration. "The Son of Man is Lord even of the Sabbath," or perhaps we might translate it "also" or "too"—"the Son of Man is Lord also of the Sabbath," "of the Sabbath too." In the former case it is the loftiness of the lordship which is Lord even of the Sabbath which is suggested; in the latter, it is the wideness of the lordship which our Lord asserts for Himself which is intimated. Both elements of significance are present, however, in either case. The emphasis in any event falls on the greatness of the authority claimed by our Lord when He declared His lordship over the Sabbath, and the term "Lord" is in the original thrust forward in the sentence, that it may receive the whole stress. This great dominion our Lord vindicates to Himself as the Son of Man, that heavenly being, whom Daniel saw coming with the clouds of heaven to set up on earth the eternal kingdom of God. Because the Sabbath was made for man, He, the Son of Man, to whom has been given dominion and glory, and a kingdom, that all peoples, nations, and languages should serve Him—who reigns by right over man and all things which concern man—is Lord also of the Sabbath. There are obviously two sides to the declaration. The Sabbath, on the one hand, is the Lord's Day. It belongs to Him. He is the Lord of it; master of it—for that is what "Lord" means. He may do with it what He will; abolish it if He chooses—though abolishing it is as far as possible from the suggestion of the passage; regulate it, adapt it to the changing circumstances of human life for the benefit of which it was made. On the other hand, just because it is the Lord's Day, it is nobody else's day. It is not man's day; it is not in the power of man. To say that the Son of Man is Lord of the Sabbath is to withdraw it from the control of men. It is to reserve to the Son of Man all authority over it. It is not man but the Son of Man who is Lord of the Sabbath.

When we wish to remind ourselves of the foundations of the Sabbath in the Word of God, it is naturally to the Decalogue that we go first. There we read the fundamental commandment which underlay the Sabbath of which our Lord asserted Himself to be the Lord, and the divine authority and continued validity of which He recognized and reaffirmed when He announced Himself Lord of the Sabbath established by it. The Ten Commandments were, of course, given to Israel; and they are couched in language that could only be addressed to Israel. They are introduced by a preface adapted and doubtless designed to give them entrance into the hearts of precisely the Israelitish people, as the household ordinances of their own God, the God to whom they owed their liberation from slavery and their establishment as a free people; "I am the Lord thy God, which have brought thee out of the land of Egypt, out of the house of bondage" [Ex. 20:2]. This intimacy of appeal specifically to Israel is never lost throughout the whole document. Everywhere it has just Israel in mind, and in every part of it it is closely adapted to the special circumstances of Israel's life. We may, therefore, read off from its texts many facts about Israel. We may learn from it, for example, that Israel was a people in which the institution of slavery existed; whose chief domestic animals were oxen and asses, not, say, horses and camels; whose religious practices included sacrificial rites; and which was about to enter into a promised land, given to it of the Lord for its possession. We may learn from it also that Israel was a people to whom the Sabbath was already known, and which needed not to be informed, but only to be reminded of it; "Remember the Sabbath day...." Nothing can be clearer, then, than that the Ten Commandments are definitely addressed to the Israelitish people and declare the duties peculiarly incumbent upon them.

Unless it be even clearer that these duties, declared thus to be peculiarly incumbent upon the Israelitish people, are not duties peculiar to that people. Samuel R. Driver describes the Ten Commandments as "a concise but comprehensive summary of the duties of the Israelite towards God and man...." It does not appear but that this is a very fair description of them. They are addressed to the Israelite. They give him a concise but comprehensive summary of his duties towards God and man. But the Israelite, too, is a man. And it ought not to surprise us to discover that the duties of the Israelite towards God and man, when summarily stated, are just the fundamental duties which are owed to God and man by every man, whether Greek or Jew, circumcision or uncircumcision, barbarian, Scythian, bond or free. Such, at all events is, in point of fact, the case. There is no duty imposed upon the Israelite in the Ten Commandments, which is not equally incumbent upon all men, everywhere. These commandments are but the positive publication to Israel of the universal human duties, the common morality of mankind.

It was not merely natural but inevitable that in this positive proclamation of universal human duties to a particular people, a special form should be given their enunciation specifically adapting them to this particular people in its peculiar circumstances; and it was eminently desirable that they should be so phrased and so commended as to open a ready approach for them to this particular people's mind and to bring them to bear with special force upon its heart. This element of particularity embedded in the mode of their proclamation, however, has no tendency to void these commandments of their intrinsic and universal obligation. It only clothes them with an additional appeal to those to whom this particular proclamation of them is immediately addressed. It is not less the duty of all men to do no murder, not to commit adultery, not to steal, not to bear false witness, not to covet a neighbor's possession, that the Israelite too is commanded not to do these things, and is urged to withhold himself from them by the moving plea that he owes a peculiar obedience to a God who has dealt with him with distinguishing grace. And it is not less the duty of all men to worship none but the one true God, and Him only with spiritual worship; not to profane His name nor to withhold from Him the time necessary for His service, or refuse to reverence Him in His representatives, that these duties are impressed especially on the heart of the Israelite by the great plea that this God has shown Himself in a peculiar manner his God. The presence of the Sabbath commandment in the midst of this series of fundamental human duties, singled out to form the compact core of the positive morality divinely required of God's peculiar people, is rather its commendation to all peoples of all times as an essential element in primary human good conduct.

It is clearly this view of the matter which was taken by our Lord. How Jesus thought of the Ten Commandments we may easily learn from His dealing with the rich young ruler who came to Him demanding: "Good Master, what shall I do to inherit eternal life?" [Luke 18:18]. "Thou knowest the commandments," our Lord replied; "if thou wouldst enter into life, keep the commandments." Nothing new is suggested by our Lord; nothing but the same old commandments which Jehovah had given Israel in the Ten Words. "Thou knowest the commandments," says He; "the commandments." They are the well-known commandments which every one in Israel knew well. "I have nothing else to say to you except what you already know..." so one of the most modern of modern commentators (Johannes Weiss) paraphrases our Lord's response; "He who would be worthy of the kingdom of God must keep the primeval commandments of God." And that no mistake might be made as to His meaning, our Lord goes on to enumerate a sufficient number of the Ten Commandments to make it clear even to persistent misunderstanding what commandments He had in mind. "Thou shalt not kill," He specifies, "thou shalt not steal, thou shalt not bear false witness, honor thy father and thy mother," and He adds, summing up as much of them as He had repeated, "Thou shalt love thy neighbor as thyself." So little does Jesus imagine that the Ten Commandments were of local and temporary obligation that He treats them as the law of the universal and eternal kingdom which He came to establish.

Nor has He left us to infer this merely from His dealing with them in such instances as this of the rich young ruler. He tells us explicitly that His mission as regards the law was, not to abrogate it, but "to fulfil it," that is to say, "to fill it out," complete it, develop it into its full reach and power. The law, He declares, in the most solemn manner, is not susceptible of being done away with, but shall never cease to be authoritative and obligatory. "For verily I say unto you,' he says, employing for the first time in the record of His sayings which have come down to us, this formula of solemn asseveration—"Verily I say unto you, till heaven and earth pass away, one jot or one tittle shall in no wise pass away from the law, till all things be accomplished" [Matt. 5:18]. So long as time endures, the law shall endure in full validity, down to its smallest details. The concluding phrase of this declaration, rendered in our Revised Version "until all things be accomplished," and perhaps even more misleadingly in the Authorized Version, "till all be fulfilled," is not a mere repetition of "till heaven and earth pass away," but means, in brief, "until all which the law requires shall be done, until no item of the law shall remain unobserved." So long as the world stands no iota of the law shall pass away—till all that it prescribes shall be performed. The law exists not to be broken or to be abrogated, but to be obeyed; not to be "undone," to employ an old English phrase, but to be "done." It is to be obeyed, and it shall be obeyed, down to the last detail; and, therefore, in no detail of it can it be set aside or safely neglected. "The thought is," remarks H. A. W. Meyer justly, that "the law will not lose its binding obligation, which reaches on to the final realization of all its prescriptions, so long as heaven and earth remain."

Now, the law of which our Lord makes this strong assertion of its ever-abiding validity, includes, as one of its prominent constituent parts, just the Ten Commandments. For, as He proceeds to illustrate His statements from instances in point, showing how the law is filled out, completed by Him, He begins by adducing instances from the Ten Commandments; "thou shalt not kill"; "thou shalt not commit adultery." It is with the Ten Commandments clearly in His mind, therefore, that He declares that no jot or tittle of the law shall ever pass away, but it all must be fulfilled.

Like Master, like disciple. There is an illuminating passage in the Epistle of James, in which the law is so adverted to as to throw a strong emphasis on its unity and its binding character in every precept of it. "For whosoever shall keep the whole law," we read, "and yet stumble in one point, he is become guilty of all" [James 2:10]. "The law is a whole," comments J. E. B. Mayor; "it is the revelation of God's will; disregard to a single point is disregard to the Law-giver, it is disobedience to God, and a spirit of disobedience breaks the law as a whole." If then, we keep the law, indeed, in general but fail in one precept, we have broken, not that precept only, but the whole law of which that precept is a portion. We might as well say, if we have broken the handle or the lip or the pedestal of some beautiful vase, that we have not broken the vase but only the handle or the lip or the pedestal of it, as to say that we have not broken the law when we have broken a single one of its precepts. Now, the matter of special interest to us is that James illustrates this doctrine from the Ten Commandments. It is the same God, he declares, who has said, thou shalt not commit adultery, and thou shalt not kill. If we do not commit adultery but kill, we are transgressors of the holy will of this God, expressed in all the precepts and not merely in one. It is obvious that James might have taken any others of the precepts of the Decalogue to illustrate his point—the fourth as well as the sixth or seventh. The Decalogue evidently lies in his mind as a convenient summary of fundamental duty; and he says in effect that it is binding on us all, in all its precepts alike, because they all alike are from God and publish His holy will.

An equally instructive allusion to the Decalogue meets us in Paul's letter to the Romans. Paul is dwelling on one of his favorite themes—love as the fulfillment of the law. "He who loveth his neighbor," he says, "hath fulfilled the law" [Rom. 13:8]. For, all the precepts of the law—he is thinking here only of our duties to our fellowmen—are summed up in the one commandment, "thou shalt love thy neighbor as thyself." To illustrate this proposition he enumerates some of the relevant precepts. They are taken from the second table of the Decalogue; "thou shalt not commit adultery, thou shalt not kill, thou shalt not steal, thou shalt not covet." Clearly the Ten Commandments stand in Paul's mind as a summary of the fundamental principles of essential morality, and are, as such, of eternal validity. When he declares that love is the fulfillment of these precepts, he does not mean, of course, that love supersedes them, so that we may content ourselves with loving our neighbor and not concern ourselves at all with the details of our conduct toward him. What he means is the precise contrary of this; that he who loves his neighbor has within him a spring of right conduct towards his neighbor, which will make him solicitous to fulfill all his duties to him. Love does not abrogate but fulfils the law.

Paul was not the originator of this view of the relation of love to the law. Of his Master before him we read; And He said, "Thou shalt love the Lord thy God with all thy heart, and with all thy soul, and with all thy mind. This is the great and first commandment. And a second is like unto it. Thou shalt love thy neighbor as thyself. On these two commandments hangeth the whole law, and the prophets" [Matt. 22:37–40]. That is to say, all the precepts of the law are but the development in detail, in the form of announced obligations, of the natural workings of love towards God and man. The two tables of the Decalogue are clearly in mind as respectively summed up in these two great commandments. And the meaning is, again, not that love to God and man supersedes the duties enumerated in these two tables, but that it urges prevailingly to their punctual and complete fulfillment. As loving our fellowmen does not so fulfill all our duty towards them that, loving them, we are free to rob and murder them; so loving God does not so fulfill our whole duty to Him that, loving Him, we are free to insult His name or deny Him the time necessary for His service. Love, again, means not the abrogation but the fulfillment of the law.

It cannot be necessary to multiply examples. Nothing could be clearer than that the Ten Commandments are treated by our Lord and the writers of the New Testament as the embodiment, in a form suited to commend them to Israel, of the fundamental elements of essential morality, authoritative for all time and valid in all the circumstances of life. All the references made to them have as their tendency, not to discredit them, but to cleanse them from the obscuring accretions of years of more or less uncomprehending and unspiritual tradition, and penetrating to their core, to throw up into high light their purest ethical content. Observe how our Lord deals with the two commandments, "thou shalt not kill, thou shalt not commit adultery," in the passage near the beginning of the Sermon on the Mount, to which we have already had occasion to allude. Everything external and mechanical in the customary application of these commandments is at once swept away; the central moral principle is seized with firmness; and this central moral principle is developed without hesitation into its uttermost manifestations. Murder, for example, is discovered in principle already in anger; and not in anger only, but even in harsh language. Adultery, in the vagrant impulses of the mind and senses; and in every approach to levity in the treatment of the marriage tie. There is no question here of abrogating these commandments, or of limiting their application. One might say rather that their applications are immensely extended, though "extended" is not quite the right word; say rather, deepened. They seem somehow to be enriched and ennobled in our Lord's hands, made more valuable and fecund, increased in beauty and splendor. Nothing really has happened to them. But our eyes have been opened to see them as they are, purely ethical precepts, declaring fundamental duties, and declaring them with that clean absoluteness which covers all the ground.

We have no such formal commentary from our Lord's lips on the fourth commandment. But we have the commentary of His life; and that is quite as illuminating and to the same deepening and ennobling effect. There was no commandment which had been more overlaid in the later Jewish practice with mechanical incrustations. Our Lord was compelled, in the mere process of living, to break His way through these, and to uncover to the sight of man ever more and more clearly the real law of the Sabbath—that Sabbath which was ordained of God, and of which He, the Son of Man, is Lord. Thus we have from Him a series of crisp declarations, called out as occasion arose, the effect of which in the mass is to give us a comment on this commandment altogether similar in character to the more formal expositions of the sixth and seventh Commandments. Among these such a one as this stands out with great emphasis: "It is lawful to do good on the Sabbath day" [Matt. 12:12]. And this will lead us naturally to this broad proclamation: "My Father worketh even until now, and I work" [John 5:17]. Obviously, the Sabbath in our Lord's view, was not a day of sheer idleness; inactivity was not its mark. Inactivity was not the mark of God's Sabbath, when He rested from the works which He creatively made. Up to this very moment He has been working continuously; and, imitating Him, our Sabbath is also to be filled with work. God rested, not because He was weary, or needed an intermission in His labors; but because He had completed the task He had set for Himself (we speak as a man) and had completed it well. "And God finished his work which he had made"; "and God saw everything that he had made, and behold it was very good" [Gen. 1:31]. He was now ready to turn to other work. And we, like Him, are to do our appointed work—"Six days shalt thou labor and do all thy work" [Ex. 20:9]—and then, laying it well aside, turn to another task. It is not work as such, but our own work, from which we are to cease on the Sabbath. "Six days shalt thou labor and do all thy work," says the commandment; or, as Isaiah puts it; "If thou turn thy foot from the Sabbath" (that is, from trampling it down) "from doing thy pleasure on my holy day" (that is the way we trample it down); and "call the Sabbath a delight, and the holy (day) of the Lord honorable; and shalt honor him, not doing thine own ways, nor finding thine own pleasure, nor speaking thine own words; then shalt thou delight thyself in the Lord; and I will make thee to ride upon the high places of the earth; and I will feed thee with the heritage of Jacob thy father; for the mouth of the Lord hath spoken it" [Isa. 58:13–14]. In one word, the Sabbath is the Lord's Day, not ours; and on it is to be done the Lord's work, not ours; and that is our "rest." As Bishop Westcott, commenting on the saying of the Lord's which is at the moment in our mind, put it, perhaps not with perfect exactness but with substantial truth; "man's true rest is not a rest from human, earthly labor, but a rest for divine heavenly labor." Rest is not the true essence of the Sabbath, nor the end of its institution; it is the means to a further end, which constitutes the real Sabbath "rest." We are to rest from our own things that we may give ourselves to the things of God.

The Sabbath came out of Christ's hands, we see then, not despoiled of any of its authority or robbed of any of its glory, but rather enhanced in both authority and glory. Like the other commandments it was cleansed of all that was local or temporary in the modes in which it had hitherto been commended to God's people in their isolation as a nation, and stood forth in its universal ethical content. Among the changes in its external form which it thus underwent was a change in the day of its observance. No injury was thus done the Sabbath as it was commended to the Jews; rather a new greatness was brought to it. Our Lord, too, following the example of His Father, when He had finished the work which it had been given Him to do, rested on the Sabbath—in the peace of His grave. But He had work yet to do, and, when the first day of the new week, which was the first day of a new era, the era of salvation, dawned, He rose from the Sabbath rest of the grave, and made all things new. As C. F. Keil beautifully puts it: "Christ is Lord of the Sabbath, and after the completion of His work, He also rested on the Sabbath. But He rose again on the Sabbath; and through His resurrection, which is the pledge to the world of the fruit of His redeeming work, He made this day the Lord's Day for His church, to be observed by it till the

Captain of its salvation shall return, and having finished the judgment upon all His foes to the very last, shall lead it to the rest of that eternal Sabbath which God prepared for the whole creation through His own resting after the completion of the heaven and the earth." Christ took the Sabbath into the grave with Him and brought the Lord's Day out of the grave with Him on the resurrection morn.

It is true enough that we have no record of a commandment of our Lord's requiring a change in the day of the observance of the Sabbath. Neither has any of the apostles to whom He committed the task of founding His church given us such a commandment. By their actions, nevertheless, both our Lord and His apostles appear to commend the first day of the week to us as the Christian Sabbath. It is not merely that our Lord rose from the dead on that day. A certain emphasis seems to be placed precisely upon the fact that it was on the first day of the week that He rose. This is true of all the accounts of His rising. Luke, for example, after telling us that Jesus rose "on the first day of the week" [Luke 24:1], on coming to add the account of His appearing to the two disciples journeying to Emmaus, throws what almost seems to be superfluous stress on that also having happened "on that very day." It is in John's account, however, that this emphasis is most noticeable. "Now, on the first day of the week," he tells us, "cometh Mary Magdalene early," to find the empty tomb. And then, a little later: "When therefore it was evening on that day, the first day of the week" [John 20:19], Jesus showed Himself to His assembled followers. The definition of the time here, the commentator naturally remarks, is "singularly full and emphatic." Nor is this all. After thus pointedly indicating that it was on the evening of precisely the first day of the week that Jesus first showed Himself to His assembled disciples, John proceeds equally sharply to define the time of His next showing Himself to them as "after eight days" [John 20:26]; that is to say it was on the next first day of the week that "his disciples were again within" and Jesus manifested Himself to them. The appearance is strong that our Lord, having crowded the day of His rising with manifestations, disappeared for a whole week to appear again only on the next Sabbath. George Zabriskie

Gray seems justified, therefore, in suggesting that the full effect of our Lord's sanction of the first day of the week as the appointed day of His meeting with His disciples can be fitly appreciated only by considering with His manifestations also His disappearances. "For six whole days between the rising day and its octave He was absent." "Is it possible to exaggerate the effect of this blank space of time, in fixing and defining the impressions received through his visits?"

We know not what happened on subsequent Sabbaths: there were four of them before the Ascension. But there is an appearance at least that the first day of the week was becoming under this direct sanction of the risen Lord the appointed day of Christian assemblies. That the Christians were early driven to separate themselves from the Jews (observe Acts 19:9) and had soon established regular times of "assembling themselves together," we know from an exhortation in the Epistle to the Hebrews. A hint of Paul's suggests that their ordinary day of assembly was on the first day of the week (1 Cor. 16:2). It is clear from a passage in Acts 20:7 that the custom of "gathering together to break bread" "upon the first day of the week" was so fixed in the middle of the period of Paul's missionary activity that though in haste he felt constrained to tarry a whole week in Troas that he might meet with the brethren on that day. It is only the natural comment to make when Friedrich Blass remarks: "It would seem, then, that that day was already set apart for the assemblies of the Christians." We learn from a passing reference in the Apocalypse (1:10) that the designation "the Lord's Day" had already established itself in Christian usage. "The celebration of the Lord's Day, the day of the Resurrection," comments Johannes Weiss, "is therefore already customary in the churches of Asia Minor." With such suggestions behind us, we cannot wonder that the church emerges from the apostolic age with the first day of the week firmly established as its day of religious observance. Nor can we doubt that apostolic sanction of this establishment of it is involved in this fact.

In these circumstances it cannot be supposed that Paul has the religious observance of the Lord's Day as the Christian Sabbath in mind, when he exhorts the Colossians to keep themselves in indifference with respect to the usages which he describes as "the shadow of the things to come," and enumerates as meat and drink and such things as festivals and new moons and Sabbath days (Col. 2:16). They have the substance in Christ; why should they disturb themselves with the shadow? He does indeed sweep away with these words the whole system of typical ordinances which he repeatedly speaks of as weak and beggarly elements of the world. In a similar vein he exclaims to the Galatians (4:10); "Ye observe days and months and seasons and years. I am afraid of you lest by any means I have bestowed labor upon you in vain." In thus emancipating his readers from the shadow-ordinances of the old dispensation, Paul has no intention whatever, however, of impairing for them the obligations of the moral law, summarily comprehended in the Ten Commandments. It is simply unimaginable that he could have allowed that any precept of this fundamental proclamation of essential morality could pass into desuetude.

He knew, to be sure, how to separate the eternal substance of these precepts from the particular form in which they were published to Israel. Turn to the Epistle to the Ephesians, sister letter to that of the Colossians, written at the same time and sent by the hand of the same messengers, and read from the twenty-fifth verse of the fourth chapter on, a transcript from the second table of the Decalogue, in its depth and universalizing touch, conceived quite in the spirit of our Lord's own comments on it. "Wherefore," says Paul, "putting away falsehood, speak ye each one truth with his neighbor; for we are members one of another." That is the form which the ninth commandment takes in his hands. "Be ye angry and sin not; let not the sun go down upon your wrath; neither give place to the devil." This is Paul's version of the sixth commandment. "Let him that stole, steal no more; but rather let him labor, working with his hands the thing that is good, that he may have whereof to give to him that hath need." That is how he commends the eighth commandment. "Let no corrupt speech proceed out of your mouth, but such as is good for edifying as the need may be, that it may give grace to them that hear." Thus Paul subtilizes the requirements of the seventh commandment.

If we wish, however, fully to apprehend how Paul was accustomed to Christianize and universalize the Ten Commandments while preserving nevertheless intact their whole substance and formal authority, we should turn over the page and read this (Eph. 6:2): "Children, obey your parents in the Lord; for this is right. Honor thy father and mother (which is the first commandment with promise) that it may be well with thee and thou mayest live long in the earth." Observe, first, how the fifth commandment is introduced here as the appropriate proof that obedience to parents is right. Having asserted it to be right, Paul adduces the commandment which requires it. Thus the acknowledged authority of the fifth commandment as such in the Christian church is simply taken for granted. Observe, secondly, how the authority of the fifth commandment thus assumed as unquestionable, is extended over the whole Decalogue. For this commandment is not adduced here as an isolated precept; it is brought forward as one of a series, in which it stands on equal ground with the others, differing from them only in being the first of them which has a promise attached to it; "which is the first commandment with promise." Observe, thirdly, how everything in the manner in which the fifth commandment is enunciated in the Decalogue that gives it a form and coloring adapting it specifically to the old dispensation is quietly set aside and a universalizing mode of statement substituted for it; "that it may be well with thee, and thou mayest live long on the earth." All allusion to Canaan, the land which Jehovah, Israel's God, had promised to Israel, is eliminated, and with it all that gives the promise or the commandment to which it is annexed any appearance of exclusive application to Israel. In its place is set a broad declaration valid not merely for the Jew who worships the Father in Jerusalem, but for all those true worshipers everywhere who worship Him in spirit and in truth. This may seem the more remarkable, because Paul, in adducing the commandment, calls special attention to this promise, and that in such a manner as to appeal to its divine origin. It is quite clear that he was thoroughly sure of his ground with his readers. And that means that the universalizing reading of the Ten Commandments was the established custom of the apostolic church.

Can we doubt that as Paul, and the whole apostolic church with him, dealt with the fifth commandment, so he dealt with the fourth? That he preserved to it its whole substance and its complete authority, but eliminated from it too all that tended to give it a local and temporary reference? And why should this not have carried with it, as it certainly seems to have carried with it, the substitution for the day of the God of Israel, who brought His people out of the land of Egypt, out of the house of bondage, the day of the Lord Jesus, who brought them out of worse bondage than that of Egypt by a greater deliverance, a deliverance of which that from Egypt was but a type? Paul would be dealing with the fourth commandment precisely as he deals with the fifth, if he treated the shadow-Sabbath as a matter of indifference and brought the whole obligation of the commandment to bear upon keeping holy to the Lord the new Lord's Day, the monument of the second and better creation.

That this was precisely what he did, and with him the whole apostolic church, there seems no room to question. And the meaning of that is that the Lord's Day is placed in our hands, by the authority of the apostles of Christ, under the undiminished sanction of the eternal law of God.

APPENDIX TWO

Review of *Keeping the Sabbath Today?* by Jay E. Adams

RYAN M. MCGRAW[1]

In 1853, the General Assembly of the Presbyterian Church (U.S.A.) declared: "A church without the Sabbath is apostate."[2] Even rivals such as R. L. Dabney and Charles Hodge were in perfect harmony with regard to Sabbath-keeping. Radical changes, however, have occurred with respect to Sabbath-keeping since the nineteenth century; and it is increasingly common today for Presbyterians to question Sabbath-keeping as outlined in the Westminster Standards. But the position advocated by Jay Adams in *Keeping the Sabbath Today?* represents a far more radical shift.

The question addressed in this book is not how Christians should keep the Sabbath, but *if* Christians should keep the Sabbath. In twenty short chapters, Adams answers this question with a decisive "no." The overarching purpose of this book is to demonstrate that the Decalogue, and the fourth commandment preeminently, are irrelevant to Christians as the standard for personal holiness. Instead, Christians should keep "the commandments of Christ" that are summarized by love (102). Keeping the Decalogue makes Christians guilty of Judaizing, who live like "Jewtiles" (85). Adams notes: "Admittedly this is a controversial volume" (ix).

---

1. This review of *Keeping the Sabbath Today?* by Jay Adams was originally published in *Puritan Reformed Journal* 1, no. 2 (July 2009): 274–81, and is reprinted with permission.

2. Thomas Peck, *The Works of Thomas Peck* (Richmond: Presbyterian Committee of Publication, 1895; repr., Edinburgh: The Banner of Truth Trust, 1999), I:195.

Every chapter of this book departs from the traditional Reformed understanding of the Sabbath as well as the law of God. As with all of Adams's works, this book is clearly written and tightly argued. These things, coupled with the fact that the name and reputation of the author make this volume attractive to many, make it necessary to rehearse in brief the arguments of each chapter.

Chapter 1 begins with a syllogism: The Sabbath is a Jewish holy day; Romans 14 and Colossians 2 demonstrate that Jewish holy days are not binding upon Christians; therefore, Adams asserts that "the Bible teaches that the Sabbath has been abolished." In chapters 2 and 3, Adams argues that the Sabbath was not changed from the seventh to the first day of the week because the Sabbath is not a creation ordinance, and that the commandments of the Decalogue are irrelevant in the New Testament unless they are repeated by Jesus and His apostles (13). Ignoring Genesis 2, Adams argues that the injunction to keep the Sabbath in Exodus 16 was not "a full-fledged Sabbath" (9), since labor was not forbidden. Neither Jews nor Gentiles were reprimanded for Sabbath-breaking before Exodus 20; therefore, the Sabbath was not binding upon anyone prior to Exodus 20 (11). In response to Adams, it is also true that polygamy was not expressly forbidden in the Old Testament, yet Christ implied that God's creation purpose for marriage was sufficient precedent to require an indissoluble bond between one man and one woman (Matt. 19:8). Concerning the Ten Commandments, Adams writes: "The removal of the fourth commandment, it seems, has played a part in destroying their arrangement as a codified group of laws" (13).

This naturally leads to chapter 4, in which Adams argues on the basis of Hebrews 3 and 4 that heaven is the only Christian Sabbath. He cites Calvin and the Heidelberg Catechism for support, and alleges that Hebrews 4 is the only New Testament passage that potentially urges Sabbath-keeping (vv. 20–22). Adams then builds his polemic against the Decalogue in chapter 5 by equating the Decalogue with the old covenant (27). He writes, "The church has made too much of the Ten Commandments. She has given this code undue prominence in her catechisms and teaching" (29). If Adams is correct, however, it is not so much that the church has given undue prominence to the Decalogue, as that she should not have given any prominence to the Decalogue. He blames this emphasis on the Law on the Puritans (29–30), yet all of the Reformers, including Luther, expounded the Decalogue, both in their creeds and in their major theological works. Moreover, the threefold division of the Law (i.e., moral, ceremonial, and judicial) was not an invention of the Puritans (as Adams assumes), but was developed in detail by Heinrich Bullinger, who predated Calvin.

The argument of chapter 6 is summarized thus: "[The Ten Commandments] were not merely a summary of the moral law. They witness to God's covenant that the people entered into at Sinai. This can hardly be doubted" (38). They were placed in the ark of the testimony, which contained the covenant document for Israel. For this reason, on the basis of Ephesians 2:15, Adams contends in chapter 7 that the Law separated Jews from Gentiles; and since Jews and Gentiles are no longer separated, the entire Law has been abolished (39). Instead of viewing the Ten Commandments as equivalent to the summary principles of obedience to God based upon the eternal character of God Himself, Adams believes there is a deeper set of abiding principles behind the Ten Commandments (43). If this is the case, what are these principles, where are they embodied, and why do they make the Decalogue irrelevant? Chapter 8 seeks to remove the example of Jesus as a basis for Sabbath-keeping, since He cannot be our example in this respect because He was under the Law in a manner that we are not (45–46).

Chapter 9 assumes that because three reasons are given in order to enforce Sabbath-keeping in the Old Testament (i.e., remembering creation, the Exodus, and that the Lord sanctifies Israel), we should conclude that a fourth reason would be added in the New Testament to replace the previous three, which is looking to rest in heaven. The abiding essence of the commandment is physical rest only. Resting one whole day in seven is irrelevant (51–54). Chapters 10 and 11 develop this argument further by arguing that the Sabbath was a sign that has been removed by the presence of the thing signified, and that the differences between Exodus 20 to Deuteronomy 5 demonstrate that there are actually "two fourth commandments," making the fourth differ from the other nine. Adams erroneously assumes that God may not use more than one reason to enforce a command, yet the apostle Paul clearly used more than one reason to enforce the fifth commandment (Eph. 6:1ff). Rather than proving that the fourth commandment is temporary, could not the additional presence of several reasons to enforce the commandment accentuate its importance? Owen referred to the fourth commandment as "the keeper of the whole first table."[3]

After asserting boldly in chapter 12 that there is "not even a hint" that the early church observed the first day of the week as the Christian Sabbath (63–64), Adams writes in chapter 13: "The main point is that in a worldwide society, a Jewish-like Sabbath *cannot* be observed" (69). He based this claim on the idea that the Sabbath command was tailored to the peculiar climate of Palestine (Ex. 35:3), and cannot be kept in lands with cooler climates dependent upon fire or electric heat. In the introduction to the book, Adams hints that it was impossible to keep the Sabbath because of the difficulty of several people maintaining an extended conversation suitable to a day of worship (ix). However, is what is possible for sinners a legitimate criterion by which to judge the binding significance of any part of God's law? Which commandment is possible for sinners to keep? Moreover, this position fails to distinguish the principles of the fourth commandment from their application. Strangely, and in seeming contradiction to chapter 12, chapter 14 asserts that it is important to gather for worship on the Lord's Day, not to keep the Sabbath, but for the sake of historic precedent only (71).

In chapters 15–16, Adams directs his attention to potential objections from James 2:8–13 and Matthew 5:17–20. He contends that James did not appeal to the law as normative for behavior, but for illustrative purposes only, stating that it is "obvious" that the

---

3. John Owen, *A Day of Sacred Rest*, in *An Exposition to the Epistle to the Hebrews* (repr., Edinburgh: Banner of Truth, 1991), II:289.

passage "has nothing to do with the survival of the Ten Command-ments" (79). This does not seem so obvious, however, since James did not cite the law to illustrate his teaching but to enforce his teaching. With respect to Matthew 5, he relegates the permanent relevance of the "Law and the Prophets" to the abiding prophetic significance of the Old Testament as fulfilled in Christ (81). The weakness of this interpretation is that it ignores that this passage serves as an introduction to Jesus' exposition of several commandments of the Decalogue as the standard of holiness for His kingdom.

In chapter 17, by using the negative example of Peter in Gala-tians 2:14, Adams attempts to establish the idea that Christians must live as Gentiles rather than as Jews (85). In this chapter, Adams's attack against Sabbatarians of every sort becomes overt: "Their deep concern is to retain—rather than abolish—most of the Jewish ele-ments of Sabbath observance so that, by keeping it intact, they may be able to live like Jews. Now, they wouldn't express it that way, of course. But that is precisely what they are doing. Evidence of this is their consistent application of Old Testament passages that explain Jewish life on the Sabbath to Christians. The fundamental question is, then, 'When it comes to Sabbath-keeping, are you living like a Jew or a Gentile?'" (88). Adams has oversimplified the issue. Peter asserts that we have spent enough of our past time living like Gen-tiles (1 Pet. 4:3). The matter of primary importance is maintaining a standard for holiness required by God: not whether that standard matches the lifestyle of Jews or of Gentiles.

In chapter 18, Adams denies that the Sabbath was ever designed to be a day of worship. He claims that there is no evidence in the Old Testament connecting corporate worship to the Sabbath (89). That the Sabbath was "holy" meant only that it was different from other days by excluding labor. This ignores the fact that objects, persons, and times designated as "holy" were "different" precisely because they were set apart exclusively to the worship and ser-vice of Jehovah (Lev. 27).[4] With respect to the command to hold

---

4. See Ryan McGraw, "Sabbath Keeping: A Defense of the Westminster Standards" (unpublished manuscript), chapter 1.

a "holy convocation" every Sabbath (Lev. 23:3), Adams arbitrarily relegates this to "fellowship and informal worship," rather than corporate gatherings (91). After addressing virtually every Reformed argument in favor of the Sabbath and the Decalogue in his last two chapters, Adams defends himself against the anticipated charge of antinomianism and concludes by asserting that rest is essential for the proper maintenance of the body.

An extensive biblical response to Adams's rejection of the Decalogue is necessary, but is beyond the scope of a book review. Among others, Robert L. Reymond has recently produced a substantial biblical defense of the position on Sabbath-keeping in the *Westminster Standards*[5] and John Owen's *Day of Sacred Rest* is an indomitable resource. At present, three observations are in order.

First, Adams provides little evidence of interacting with the historic theology of the church despite his claim that "for many years I voraciously devoured every book about the Sabbath that I could get my hands on" (back cover). His inaccuracies concerning the origin of the threefold division of the law have already been noted. On page 6, he cites Philip Schaff's assertion that all of the Reformers taught that the Sabbath was abrogated. Heinrich Bullinger's treatment of the fourth commandment in his *Decades* is sufficient to disapprove this assertion. Sometimes Adams's references to the historical documents are misleading. Twice he cites the second half of Lord's Day 38 of the Heidelberg Catechism, while omitting the first half (20, 68). The first half of the question requires corporate worship on the Sabbath, placing special emphasis upon Christian education. By citing only the second half of the question, Adams gives the false impression that the catechism supports his contention that the weekly Sabbath has been abrogated. Adams has also exaggerated the diversity of opinion over Sabbath-keeping in the history of the Reformed church. The Westminster divines possessed enough unity over the

---

5. Robert L. Reymond, "Lord's Day Observance," in *Contending for the Faith: Lines in the Sand that Strengthen the Church* (Fearn, Ross-shire, U.K.: Christian Focus Publications, 2005), 165–86.

Sabbath to include it in their confession and catechisms. Presbyterians have been united over these principles until relatively recently. A century ago most disputes about the Sabbath in Presbyterian circles concerned application. By contrast, most contemporary disputes about the Sabbath concern principles. By condemning Sabbatarians as Judaizers, Adams has implicitly condemned the entire Reformed tradition. This includes all Sabbatarians, whether "strict" or "loose."

Second, Adams is a Presbyterian minister, yet his complete rejection of the Decalogue effectively eliminates over one-third of the Presbyterian Standards. In writing this book, one of his purposes was to enable Presbyterian ministers who reject the Sabbath to take their ordination vows "with greater confidence" (x). The means by which he does so, however, have brought him (and those who follow him) well beyond the realm of Reformed orthodoxy. Every man is answerable only to God and must conform his conscience to God's Word, whatever the cost. Yet a Presbyterian minister should take pause when he adopts a position that virtually overthrows the historic Reformed understanding of the relationship between the law and the gospel, as well as between the Old Testament and the New. As a bare minimum, creeds and confessions that have stood the test of time deserve critical sympathy.

Third, Adams represents Sabbath-keeping as a joyless drudgery contrary to Christ's commandment to love. Even the cover of the book presents a family that looks as miserable as possible. May God prevent His people from depicting obedience to any of His commandments as joyless! God expects His people to keep His law carefully and exactly. The love of Christ demands no less (2 Cor. 5:14–15). It is only as believers keep the Ten Commandments *as* the law of Christ, sent from the hand of Christ, that His commandments are not burdensome. What should be more joyful than one day in seven filled with corporate and private worship, spiritual conversation, celebration of the resurrection of Christ, and longing for His second coming? In a time when it is increasingly common for the church to negate all distinctions between the worship of God and everything else in life, Adams's position on the Sabbath is the natural outcome. The fact that *Keeping the Sabbath Today?* should be written by a contemporary leader in the Reformed community ought to call Reformed believers to reevaluate, and return to, the biblical foundations of the relationship between the law and the gospel.

SCRIPTURE INDEX

2 Corinthians

3:13	88
4:4	80
4:6	161
5:6	145
5:7	162
5:14–15	189
5:21	53
12:2	152
12:4	152

Galatians

2:14	187
3:7	60
3:29	60
4:4–5	94
4:10	179
5:3	128
5:4	128

Ephesians

2:8–9	130
2:15	185
2:18	99
3	130
4:24	139
4:29	82, 84
5:1	95, 133, 139
5:16	80
6:1ff	186
6:2	180

Philippians

2:12–13	136
3:4–6	67
3:7–9	130
3:20	91
3:21	151, 154
4:18–21	70

Colossians

1	122
1:20	154
2	184
2:16	42, 179
3	80
3:1–2	80
3:2	90
3:10	139
3:16	20
3:23	28
3:23–24	58

1 Timothy

1:13	67
6:16	152
6:17	80

2 Timothy

3:16	23

Titus

3:4–7	130
3:5	54

Hebrews

3–4	184
4:1–11	146–51
4:20–22	184
9:14–16	122
9:15–17	12
12:7	35
13:5–6	34
13:20	13

James

1:25	95
2:5–13	98
2:8–13	186